Cameo Incrustation: The Great Sulphide Show

Other books from Paperweight Press:

Sulphides—The Art of Cameo Incrustation by Paul Jokelson
Classic French Paperweights by Edith Mannoni
The Art of the Paperweight—Perthshire by Lawrence H. Selman
The Art of the Paperweight—Saint Louis by Gérard Ingold
Identifying Antique Paperweights—Millefiori by George Kulles
Identifying Antique Paperweights—Lampwork by George Kulles
The Purloined Paperweight by P. G. Wodehouse
The Encyclopedia of Glass Paperweights by Paul Hollister
Collectors' Paperweights—Price Guide and Catalogue

Coming soon:

The Art of the Paperweight—Baccarat
The Art of the Paperweight

For more information, write **Paperweight Press, Box 1000, Santa Cruz, CA 95061**

Cameo Incrustation: The Great Sulphide Show

The Corning Museum of Glass
Corning, New York
April 21 – October 23, 1988

A loan exhibition presented by the New York-New Jersey Paperweight Collectors Association
Dr. Julius Tarshis, President

Guest curators:
Paul Jokelson
Dena K. Tarshis

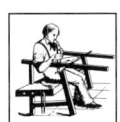

PAPERWEIGHT PRESS   SANTA CRUZ, CALIFORNIA

Cover:

1. A pair of monumental cut glass vases, mounted in gilded bronze, each baluster-form vessel deeply cut, the central circular panel enclosing an enameled foil multicolored bouquet of flowers. Baccarat, circa 1830.

This edition is limited to 2000 copies, of which one hundred copies have been specially bound in cloth and numbered.

Copyright © 1988 by Paperweight Press

All rights reserved. No part of this book may be reproduced or utilized in any form or by any means, electronic or mechanical, including photocopying, recording or by any information storage and retrieval systems, without permission in writing from the Publisher.

Set in Trump Mediæval using Aldus PageMaker

Library of Congress Cataloging-in-Publication Data

Jokelson, Paul, 1905–
    Cameo incrustation.

    Bibliography: p. 40
    1. Sulphides (Art)—Exhibitions.   I. Tarshis, Dena K.   II. New York-New Jersey Paperweight Collectors Association.   III. Corning Museum of Glass.   IV. Title.
NK5440.S8J58   1988   748.2   88-5829
ISBN 0-933756-14-3

FOREWORD

The word "sulphides" doesn't convey much to many people. Why would anyone become passionate about owning anything with such a prosaic name? The reason, I hope, will become clear as you read through this catalogue and look at the illustrations.

Typically, sulphides are elegant portraits of famous people or religious figures, and the molds were prepared by the leading sculptors and medalists of their day. The subjects include revolutionary symbols, war heroes, kings, queens, and presidents, immortalized at the peak of their popularity in a union of glass and ceramics. Many were probably personal mementos; there are tumblers and plaques meant to be displayed, and romantic subjects expressing love and devotion.

Sulphides can be magical. Finely detailed white ceramic plaques were encased in molten crystal and fashioned into elegant, elaborately cut and molded objects that were meant to impress. (They still do.) The magic is that the white ceramic material usually looks silvery. The reason is simple: Air trapped between the molten glass and the ceramic reflects light, making the surface of the plaque glisten as if it had a silvery coating.

One of the reasons that so many collectors find sulphides interesting is that identifying the portraits is not always simple. Although once immediately recognizable, many portraits defy identification today. Even the history of sulphides is not fully known. We don't know for sure when, where, or by whom the first ones were made. We don't even know why they were called "sulphides" or "sulfures." Furthermore, we aren't certain how to identify the manufacturer of most of the objects. The maker of the sulphide did not necessarily encase it in glass; perhaps he did so only rarely. French sulphides for example, are known to have been used by Bohemian and English glassmakers. The field is wide open for significant discoveries.

We hope that this catalogue and the exhibition it documents will attract many new devotees to the collecting and studying of sulphides.

Dwight P. Lanmon
Director
The Corning Museum of Glass

CAMEO INCRUSTATION

The art of glyptics, or carving on colored hard stones, is probably one of the oldest known to man. Gem engraving was a major art in ancient times. A phenomenon in Hellenistic glyptics was the emergence of the portrait gem. Alexander the Great is believed to have had a personal portraitist. When depicting the Conqueror of the World in stone, the engraver gave him a likeness to Zeus. Alexander's successors, Ptolemy III, Arsinoe III, and Mithridates VI, were likewise portrayed on gems with attributes of deities. There existed great competition between distinguished Roman families striving to outshine one another, which served to encourage the genre of glyptics.

Cameo engraving became so fashionable that satirists spoke in jest of the Roman dandies wearing not just one ring on each finger, but one on almost every knuckle. The status of the gem engraver reached such a high artistic level that the artist adopted the custom of engraving his name on his work.

The difficulty of engraving gems, indeed a laborious technique, was somewhat simplified by engraving on softer mollusk shells, which exposed white reliefs against darker grounds. The Renaissance saw Antonio Pisanello master the production of small portrait medallions in the fifteenth century and Benvenuto Cellini likewise in the sixteenth century, although in a metallic medium. The eighteenth century saw Giovanni Pichler, John Flaxman, and James Tassie as masters of portrait medallions.

James Tassie (1734–1799), a Scotsman, was famous throughout Europe as a copier of thousands of engraved gems. His own examples of the precious stones were so convincing that his gems were frequently sold to notable collectors as original by fraudulent dealers. In 1763 he invented a vitreous white paste which developed into a substance used to cast wax portraits and gems. The ingredients were fused to a thick consistency (pâte de verre), impressed in a plaster-of-paris mold, and then polished. He was able to vary the color from transparent to opaque. The glass paste was used as a medium for modelling his portrait miniatures. They were mostly oval-shaped and generally in profile. They measured 4 by 3-1/2 inches and bore names of sitters and dates on the truncation. In his earlier efforts, his paste portraits were affixed to a background of glass that was colored by the insertion of paper.

In time Tassie was able to master the technically more difficult process of casting these portraits in a single piece. Problems with the annealing process made this quite complicated.

He proudly exhibited his portrait medallions in paste at the Royal Academy from 1769 to 1791 and was employed by the great firm of Wedgwood and Bentley for several years.

The ancient "Portland Vase" found in the sixteenth century, now in the British Museum, was also a prelude to cameo incrustation. The vase was made of glass and ornamented with white opaque upon a dark blue transparent ground. Giovanni Pichler, previously mentioned as a gem engraver, had made molded copies of the Portland vase at Rome. Apsley Pellatt, along with the Marquis of Exeter and James Byrnes, possessed copies of the vase.

At the time the vase was offered for sale to the Duchess of Portland for 1800 guineas, it occurred to Josiah Wedgwood that, since this was such a rare and celebrated piece, there would be a market for good quality copies. It proved to be a correct assumption, and according to records, Apsley Pellatt attempted to have exclusivity in dealing with the vases. Pellatt had been a keen middleman in the marketing of fine Wedgwood wares and also had a fine personal collection of works by the first Josiah and by the Wedgwood and Bentley partnership.

Apparently the Bohemians and the French were the first to encrust small figures of grayish clay in glass in the late eighteenth century. The results were generally poor, as the cameos would not adhere to the glass due to the absence of silicates. The other difficulty in the process was that the cameos had to have a fusion point above that of the glass employed, otherwise they would be distorted. It was also necessary for the cameos to be able to expand and contract.

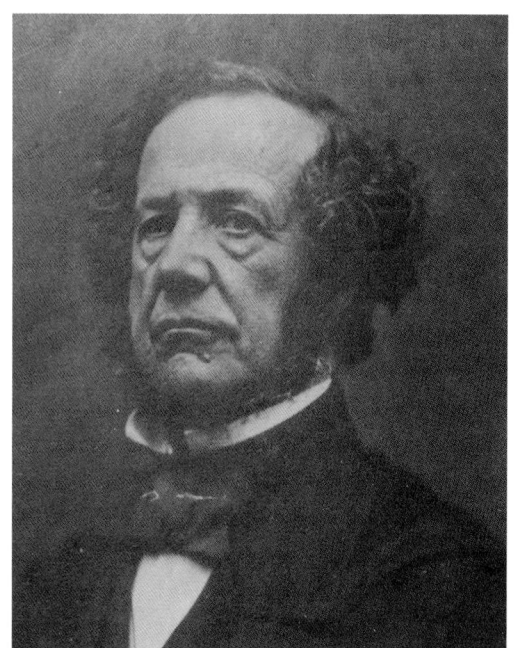

Apsley Pellatt

The glassmakers of France and England were greatly concerned about the chemistry of art. A correspondence ensued between the artists, e.g., Bontemps and d'Artigues in France, Pellatt and Hartley in England; a sort of erudite society being formed.

The Frenchman Barthelmy Desprez produced cameo portraits in a white porcellaneous material, and by the early nineteenth century was able to encase them in crystal. Another Frenchman, Boudon de Saint-Amans, also greatly improved the art. The French succeeded in encrusting several medallions of Bonaparte, which were sold at an enormous price.

Apsley Pellatt was deeply interested in the process, which he termed "Crystallo Ceramie" or cameo incrustation. The French term was *sulfures.* Pellatt took out a patent in 1819 and left an account of his work. His work must be identified on stylistic grounds, since much of it was unsigned. Pellatt's shapes as well as his style of cutting bear a great similarity to the Anglo-Irish glass of the nineteenth century. In rare instances, the cameos were painted before being fused with the glass. Specimens of these incrustations have been exhibited in decanters, candelabras, chimney ornaments, and many other small objects.

The Baccarat factory specialized in armorials, crests and monograms and set them in gold and colored glass in tableware. These luxury goods were especially favored by Czar Alexander I of Russia.

The introduction of toilet and perfume bottles created a demand for colored glass. Colors such as blue, yellow, green and amethyst were used, although dark colors were avoided due to the loss of light. The outer wall of glass behind the sulphide was generally elaborately cut in order to mask the refraction of light, while glass covering the sulphide was generally colorless.

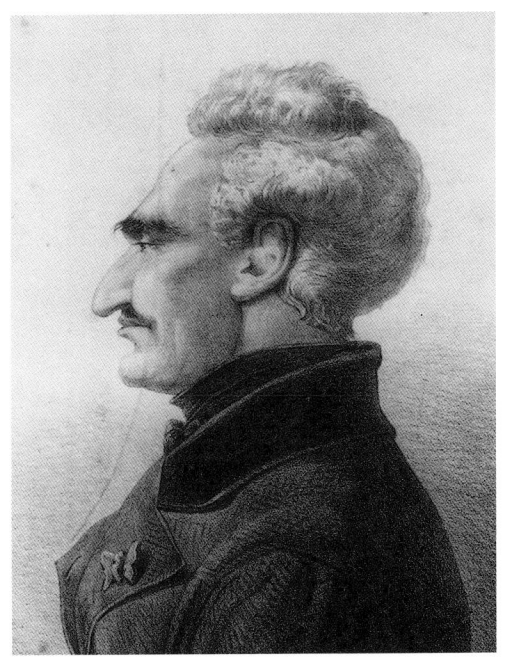

Pierre Honoré Boudon de Saint-Amans

The study of sulphide-decorated glassware of the early nineteenth century leaves no doubt that this art form was well advanced prior to the classic period of paperweight making (1840–1860).

Eventually, the production of sulphides extended to Spain, Portugal, Germany, and the United States, as well as France, England and Bohemia.

The great French glass factories of Baccarat, Saint Louis, and Clichy incorporated the use of sulphides in the manufacture of paperweights by the 1840s. Toward the end of the nineteenth century, production fell into decline, not to be revived until 1951 by the Baccarat and the Saint Louis factories.

With renewed interest in this art form, *Sulphides—The Art of Cameo Incrustation* was published by Paul Jokelson. This still serves as the definitive treatise on the subject.

Sulphides are eagerly sought by collectors. Queen Mary had many such objects in her private museum. Other notable collections include the Applewhaite-Abbott collection, sold at Sotheby's in 1952, and the Guggenheim collection sold in 1960. The display of virtuosity in the manufacture of sulphides serves as an allure for collectors. Even those whose interests are only academically oriented are fascinated with the identification of the subjects encased in glass.

The most comprehensive public collection of sulphides is housed at the Corning Museum of Glass. Examples from virtually every country that produced them is represented. The museum, therefore, serves as a most suitable venue for a loan exhibition of sulphides.

I would like to express my gratitude to Volina V. Lyons, archivist at Sotheby's, New York, for her assistance in preparing the descriptions.

Dena K. Tarshis

2 & 3. Two door plates with cameo figures of Temperance and Fortitude, two of the four cardinal virtues (the other two are Justice and Prudence). Apsley Pellatt, circa 1820.
A plate similar to no. 3 is illustrated in Apsley Pellatt, *Memoir on the Origin, Progress, and Improvement of Glass Manufactures*, plate G, fig. 16.
Exhibited: Paperweights: "Flowers which clothe the meadows," 1978, Corning Museum of Glass, #332 & 333.

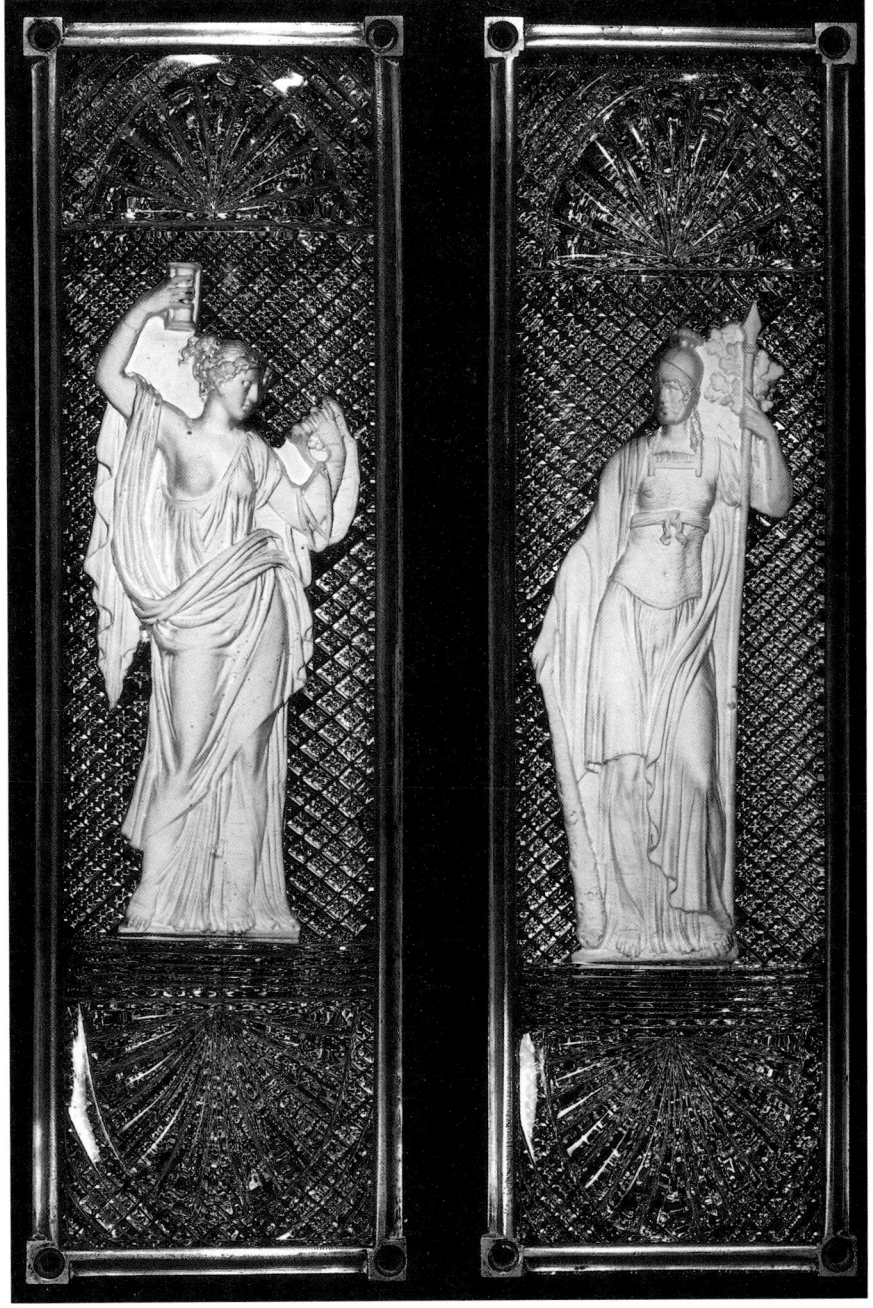

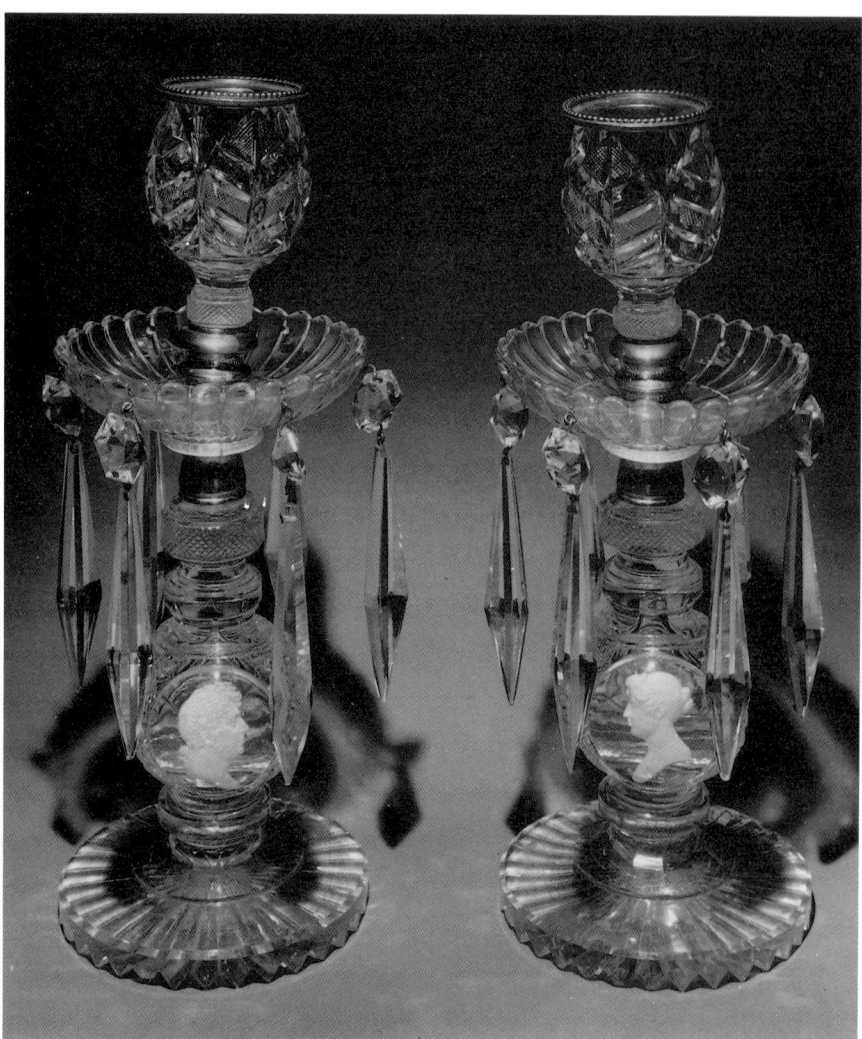

4. A pair of lustres enclosing portrait profiles of George IV (1762–1830) and Queen Victoria (1819–1901). Apsley Pellatt, circa 1840–1860.

Opposite page:

5. A pair of candlesticks, enclosing statuettes of "La Frileuse" (after Houdon), the diamond-cut thistle-shaped nozzles supported on octagonal diamond-panelled stems, resting on circular footings with basal radial cutting. Apsley Pellatt, circa 1820.
A candlestick of similar form is illustrated in Pellatt, *Memoir . . . of Glass Manufactures*, plate C, fig. 9.

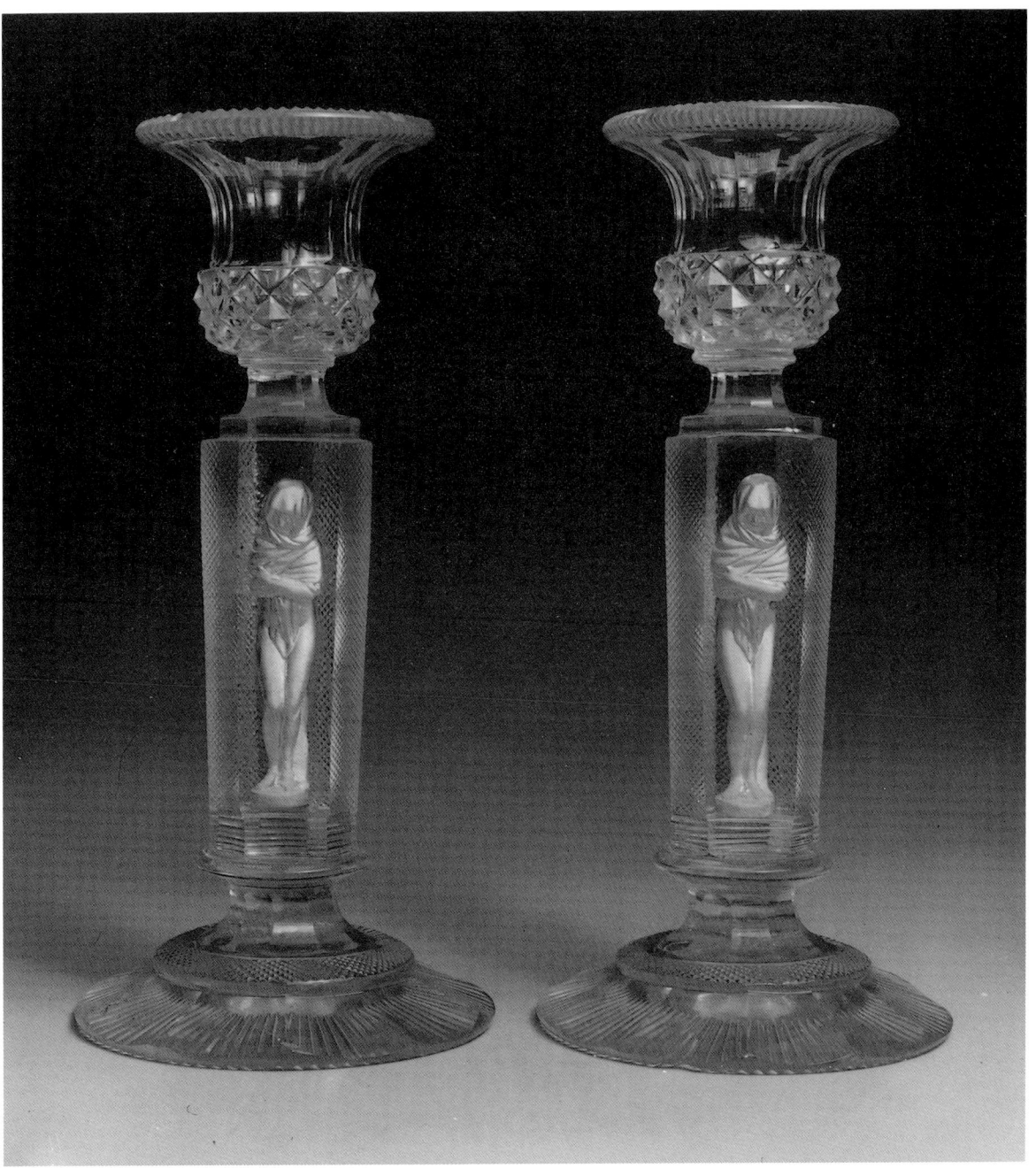

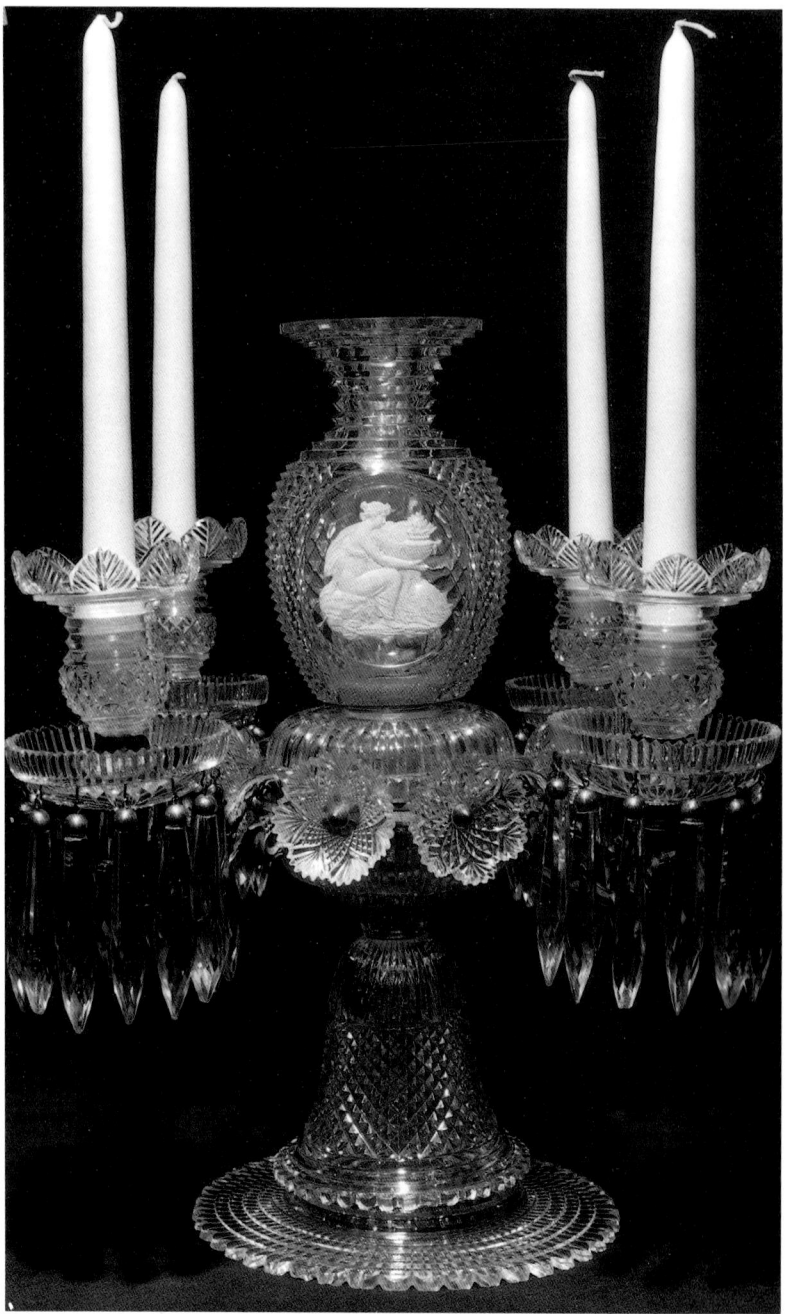

6. A massive cut glass table centerpiece, the urn-shaped central ornament set with a classical figure, probably "Sacrifice to Hygeia," the whole with hobnail and diamond cutting, containing four metal arms. Apsley Pellatt, circa 1820.

A candelabrum or girandole of similar form is illustrated in Apsley Pellatt's *Memoir . . . of Glass Manufactures,* plate F, fig. 12. He states that the center vase was intended to hold real or artificial flowers.

Opposite page:

7. A cut glass candelabrum, the hobnail-cut stem set with a profile portrait of George IV in the guise of a Roman emperor, the reverse with profile portrait of William Pitt (1759–1806). Apsley Pellatt, circa 1820.

A similar candelabrum is described in the sale of Mrs. Applewhaite-Abbott, May 30, 1952, Sotheby's, London.

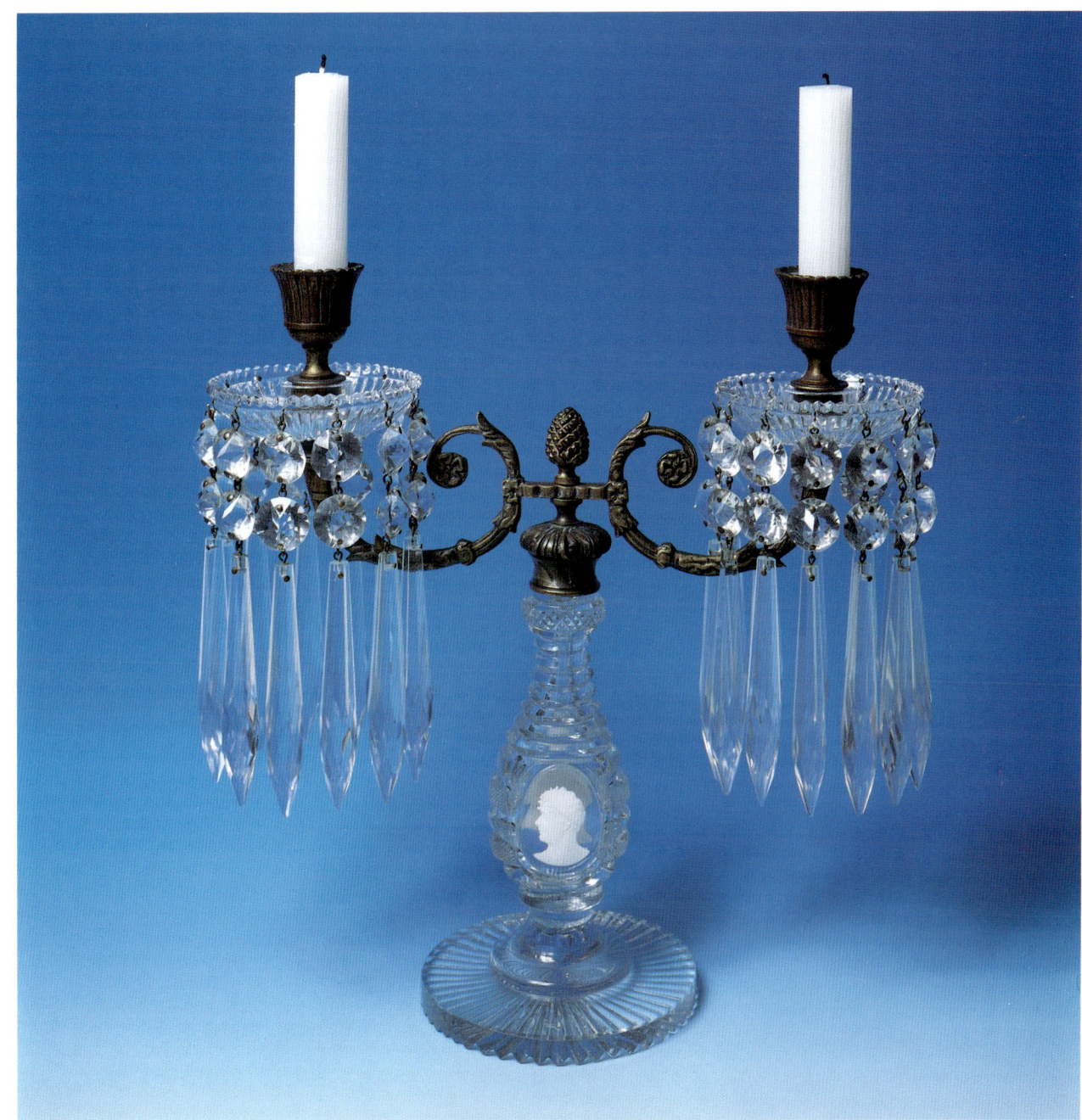

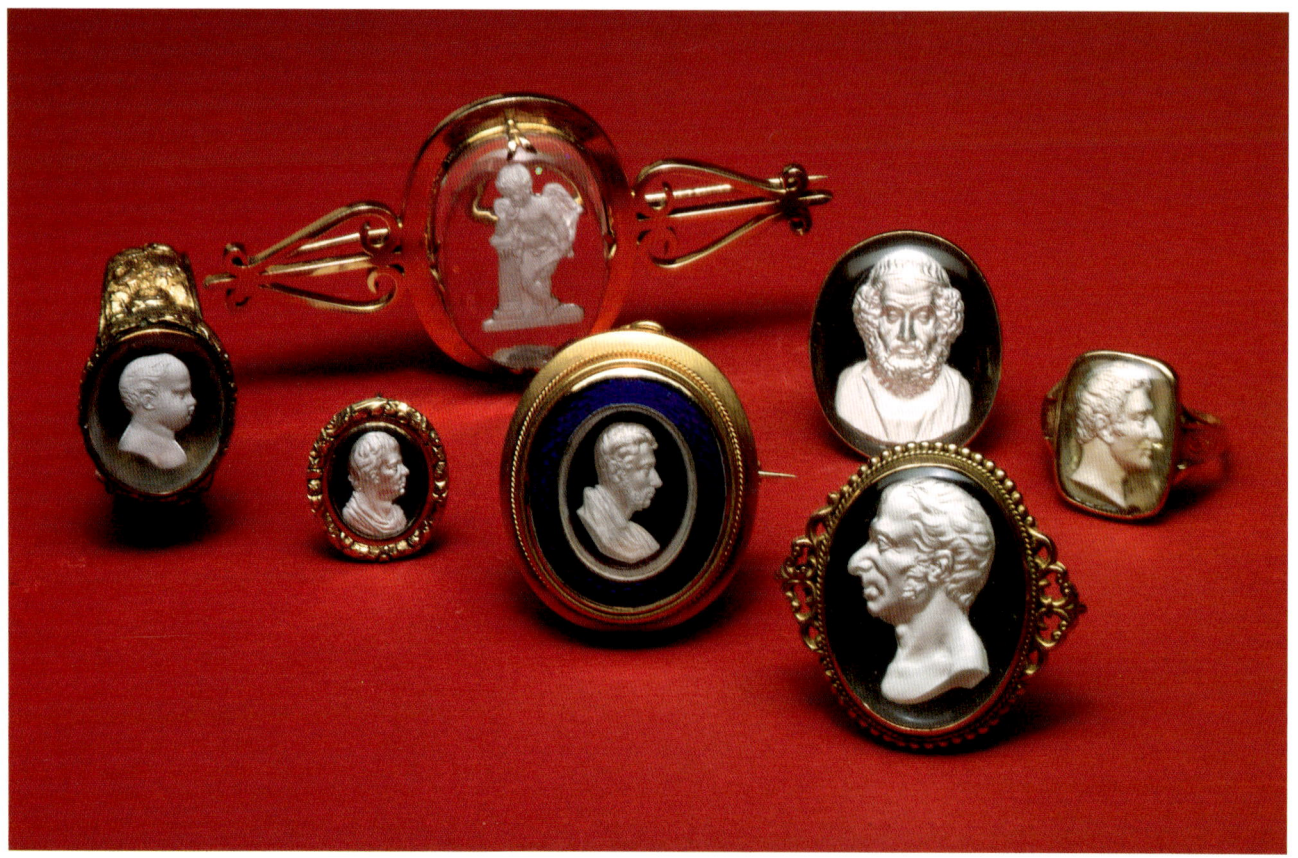

8. A fob of Pinchbeck metal enclosing a portrait profile of Napoléon II (1811–1832), the "King of Rome." English, circa 1825.
9. A gold brooch, the lozenge-shaped gold mounting enclosing a putto figure. English, circa 1810.
10. A ring, the gold mounting enclosing a portrait of Homer. English, circa 1810.
11. A ring, the gold mounting enclosing a portrait profile of Arthur Wellesley, first duke of Wellington (1769–1852). English, circa 1810.
12. A brooch, the gold mounting enclosing a profile portrait of a man, possibly Denis Diderot (1713–1784). English, circa 1830.
13. A brooch, the gold mounting containing a sulphide of a man, possibly Dr. William Stukeley, enclosed by a blue enamel frame. English, circa 1840.
14. A small brooch, the gold mounting enclosing a profile portrait of Sir Walter Scott (1771–1832). English, circa 1810.

15. A demi-parure, consisting of a necklace and earrings, the portrait profiles on lilac ground, enclosed in gold and enamel mountings. Apsley Pellatt, circa 1850.
Literature: Jokelson, *Sulphides*, fig. I.

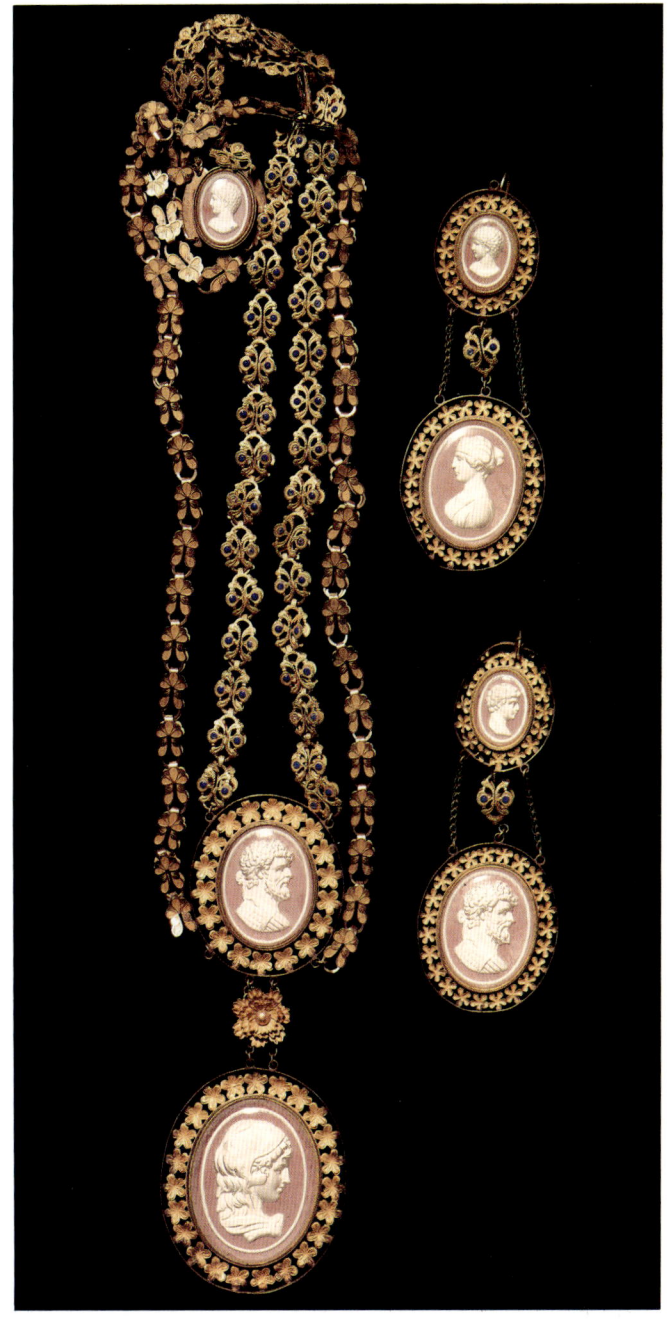

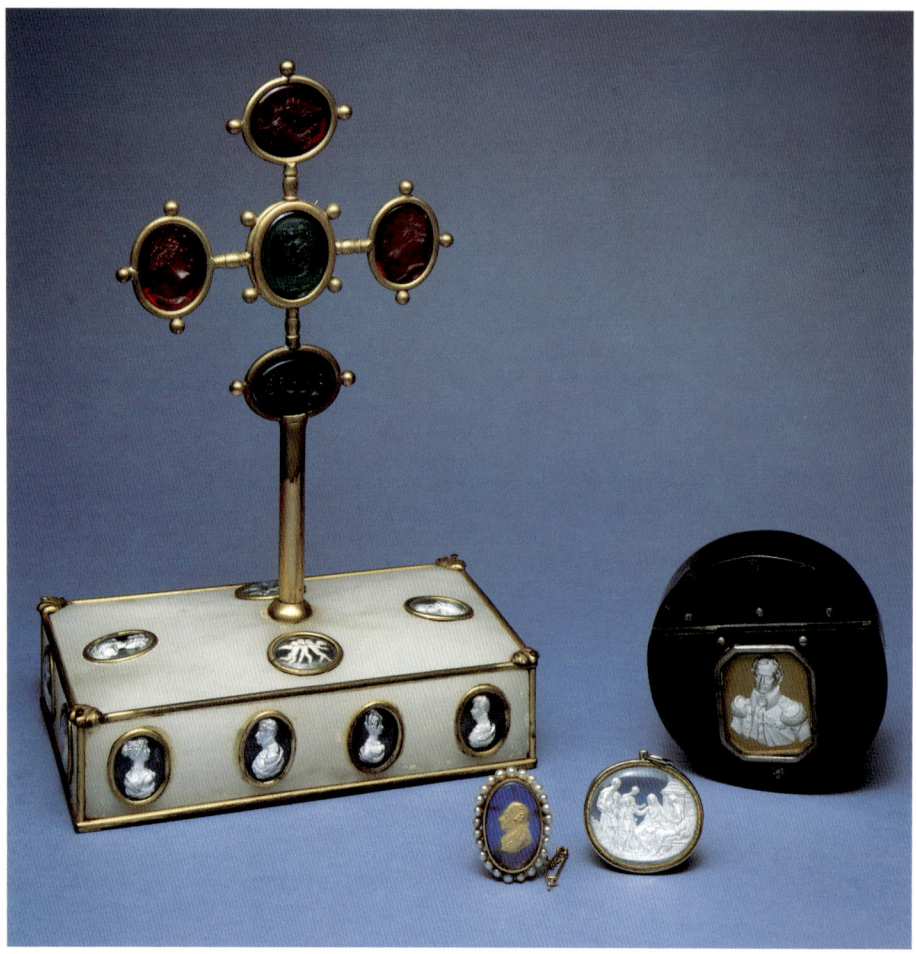

The objects on this page (nos. 16–19) are sulphide imitations. The composition cameos are not completely enclosed in glass, but rather applied from the reverse side.

16. A mantel ornament, the cruciform upper portion containing glass paste intaglios of classical figures, some signed in classical Greek; the base enclosing family portraits and billing doves. The doves suggest the possibility that this ornament was executed to commemorate a marriage.

The cameo family portraits include members of English and Russian nobility, while the center glass paste intaglio depicts Victory crushing an eagle, symbolic of Napoléon. It has also been suggested that the object was produced to commemorate the victory of England and Russia over Napoléon.

English, circa 1840–1850.

17. A circular papier-maché snuff box, containing a cameo of Friedrich Wilhelm III of Prussia (1770–1840). English, possibly Allen and Moore, circa 1854.

18. A pendant enclosing a cameo of a classic scene, gold mounting, signed *BURCH*. Edward Burch (1730–1815) worked for James Tassie and was the master of Nathaniel Marchant. English, circa 1830.

19. A small oval brooch containing a gilded cameo of Frederick the Great (1712–1786) on blue-tinted glass, the gold mounting encircled by a border of pearls. English, circa 1820.

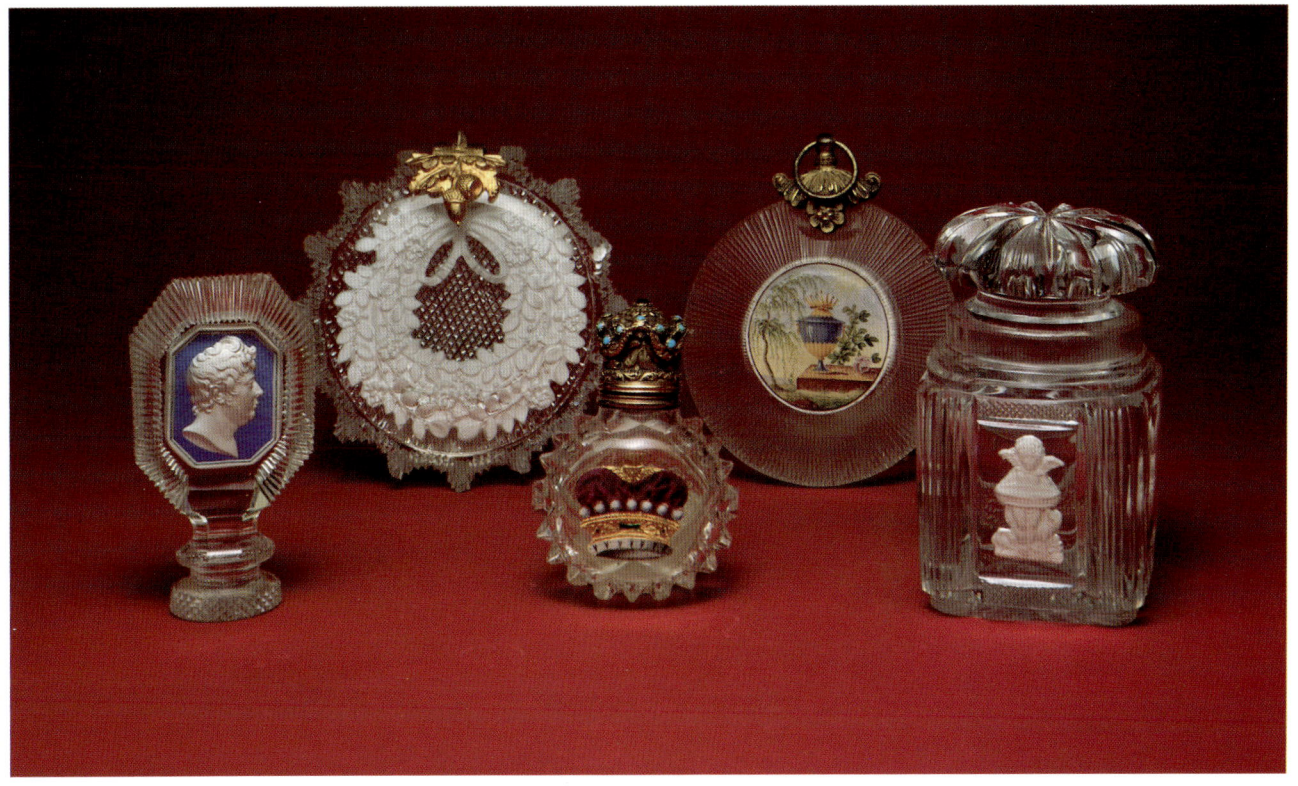

20. A double seal, the central medallion set with a profile portrait of George III on blue ground, the reverse enclosing a classical figure of "The Dying Gaul." Apsley Pellatt, circa 1810.

21. A circular plaque enclosing a wreath composed of foliage and flowers tied together by a bow, diamond-cut base. Apsley Pellatt, circa 1820.

22. A double plaque enclosing a painted medallion depicting a memorial scene, the reverse side containing a portrait of Princess Charlotte (1796–1817). Apsley Pellatt, circa 1815–1830.
Literature: Jokelson, *Sulphides,* figs. 3 and 4.

23. A four-panel bottle, enclosing a putto figure, a bouquet, and profile portraits of the Duke of Wellington and George Washington. Apsley Pellatt, circa 1820.

24. An enameled foil scent bottle containing a medallion of a crown, the gold stopper set with various stones. Apsley Pellatt, circa 1820–1830.

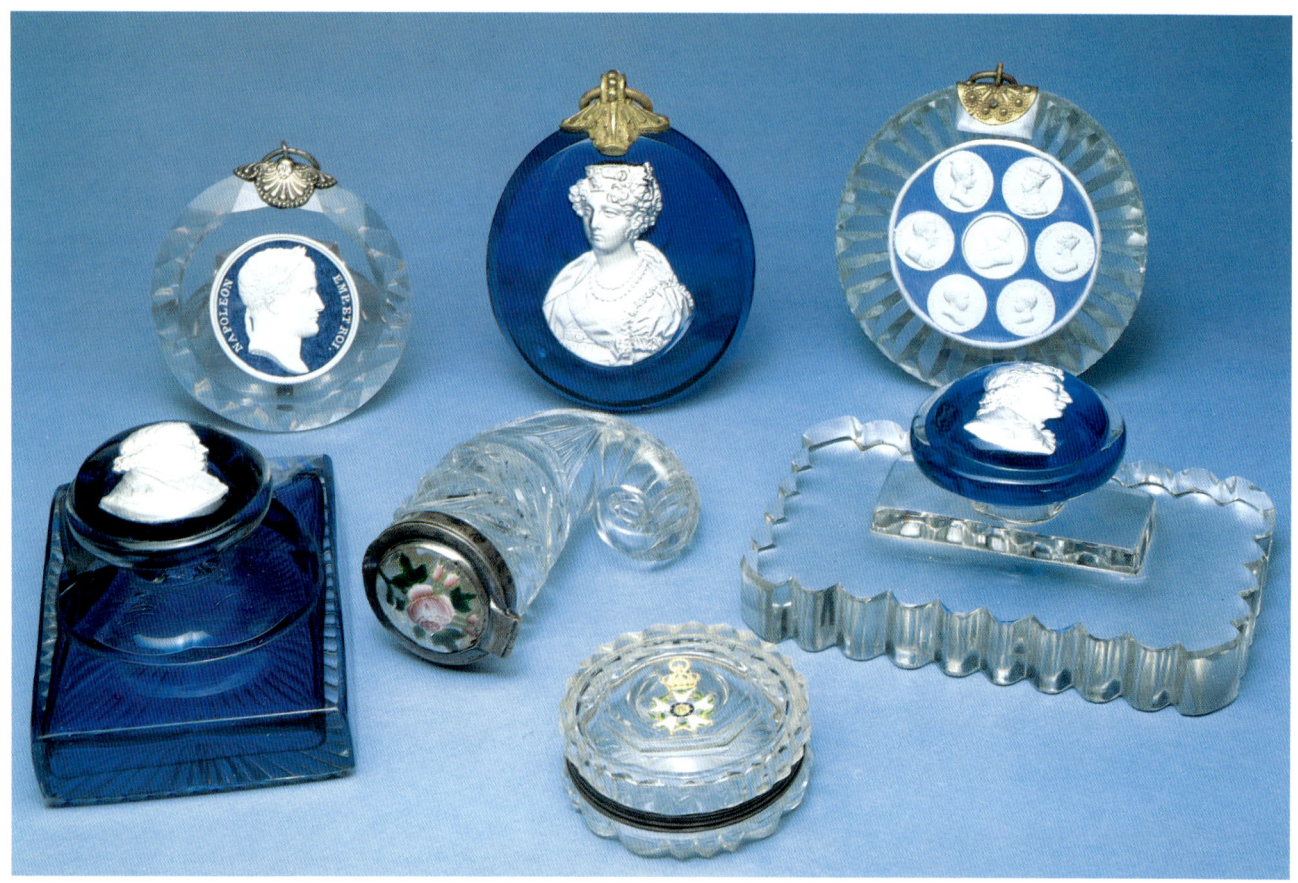

25. A circular plaque enclosing a wafer-shaped medallion of Napoléon I, on blue ground, inscribed *NAPOLEON EMP. ET ROI.* Baccarat, circa 1824.

26. A circular plaque enclosing a profile portrait of Maria-Thérèse de Bourbon, duchesse d'Angoulême (1778–1851) on a blue-tinted ground. Baccarat, circa 1820.
Literature: Jokelson, *Sulphides,* fig. XXV.

27. A circular plaque with molded portraits of Charles X (1757–1836) and six members of the royal family on a blue ground. Baccarat, circa 1824.
Literature: Jokelson, *Sulphides,* fig. XXV.

28. A letter press with profile portrait of Martin Luther (1483–1546) on encased blue-tinted ground, stepped form. Radial cutting on the base. Baccarat, circa 1825.

29. An enameled foil snuff mull, the cut glass mull containing a lid with an enameled foil inclusion of a rose. Baccarat, circa 1820–1840.

30. A letter press, the clear glass base with a circular profile portrait of Marie-Joseph de Chénier (1764–1811), on encased blue-tinted ground, stepped form. Baccarat, circa 1825.

31. An enameled foil patch box, the lid depicting the Legion of Honor. Baccarat, circa 1830.

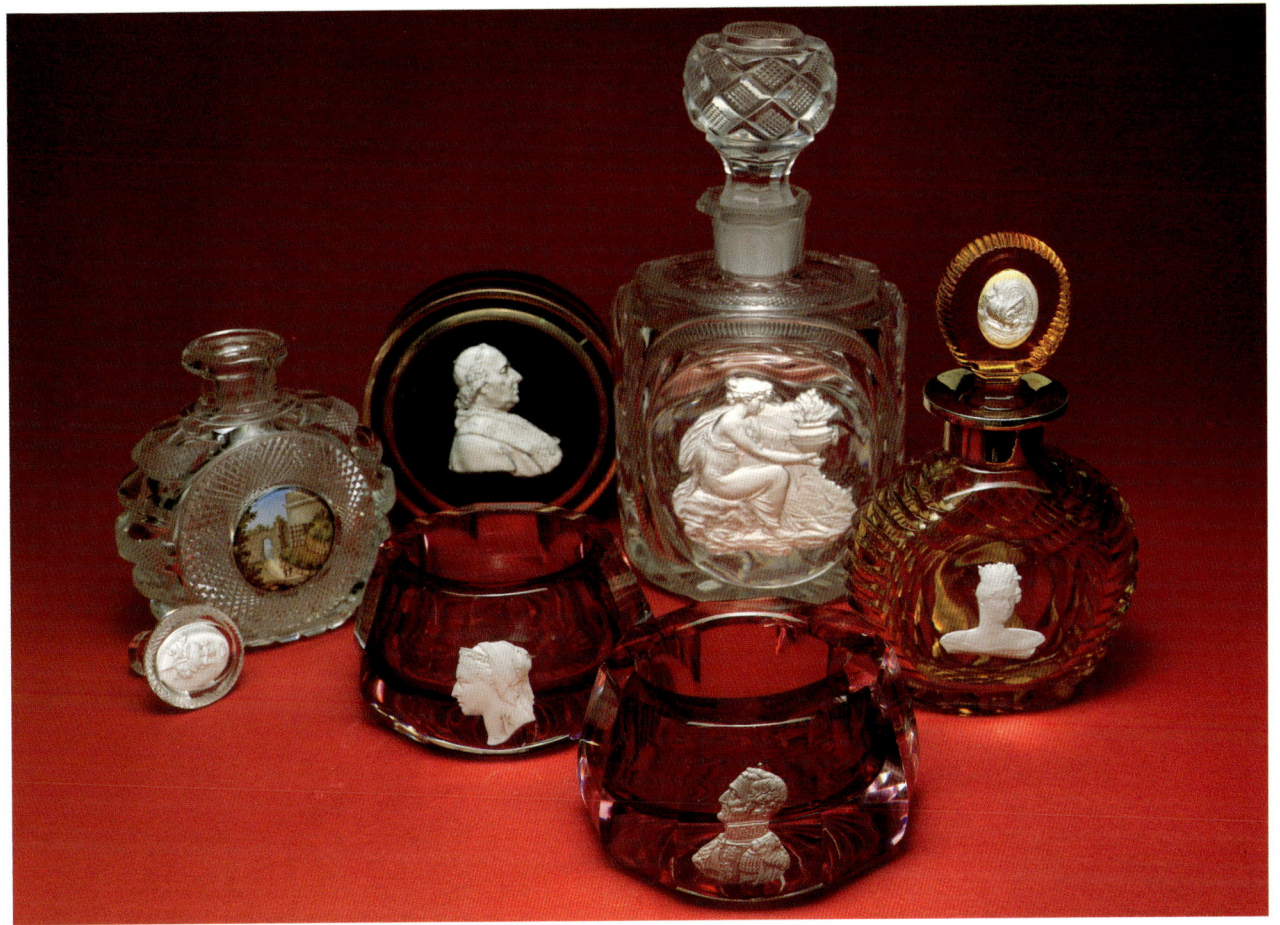

32. A scent bottle enclosing a painted landscape medallion, stopper with allegorical figure. Apsley Pellatt, circa 1820.

33. A snuff box, the tortoiseshell and gold circular box enclosing a portrait profile of a man in ecclesiastical garb. Apsley Pellatt, circa 1830–1840.

34. A large flask and stopper with central portrait medallion depicting a classical figure, probably Hygeia, diamond cutting on flask and stopper. Apsley Pellatt, circa 1820.

35. A topaz-tinted bottle and stopper, with central portrait medallion of Princess Charlotte. The stopper with double sulphides containing putti figures, the bottle with hobnail and diamond cutting. Apsley Pellatt, circa 1820.

36. A pair of salts, enclosing profile portraits of Queen Victoria and the Duke of Wellington on cranberry-tinted grounds. Probably Apsley Pellatt, circa 1840–1860.
Literature: Jokelson, *Sulphides*, fig. IX.

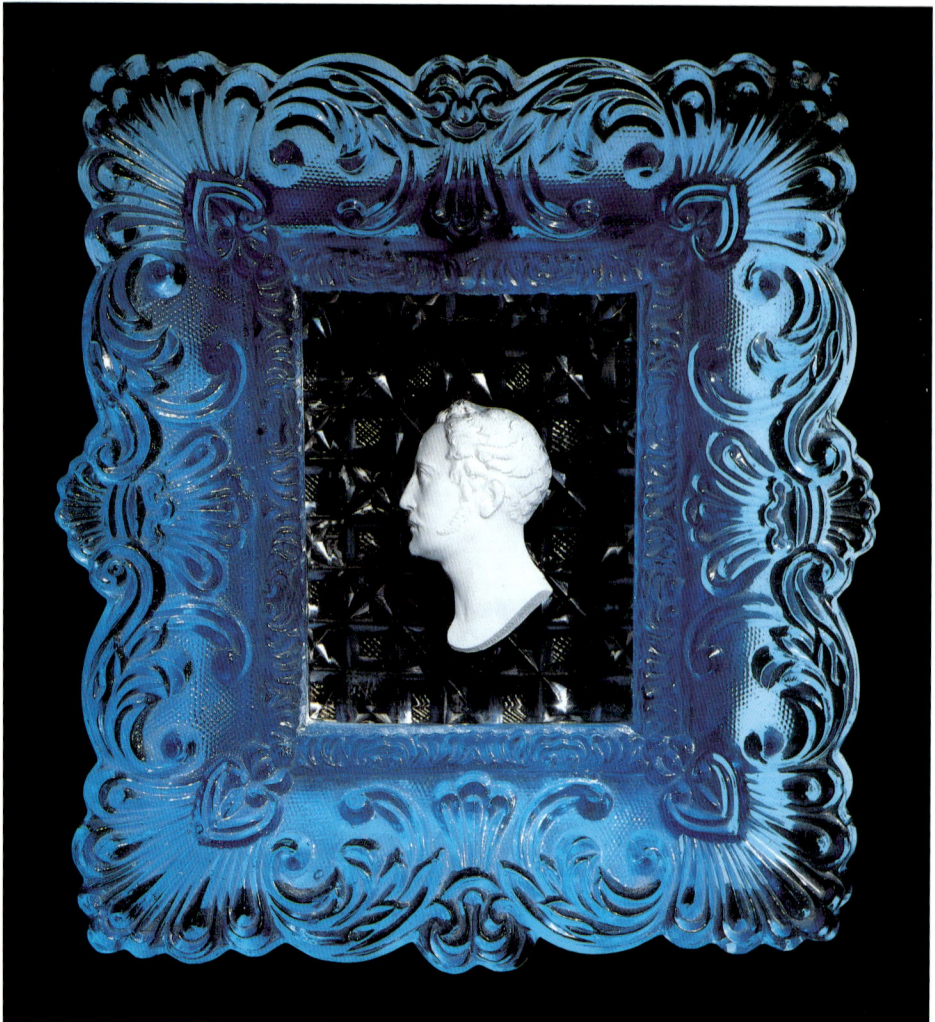

37. A portrait plaque, the clear glass enclosing a portrait profile of Czar Nicholas I (1796–1855) by A. Pickel, surrounded by a blue pressed glass frame. Bakhmetief at Nikolskoie, circa 1830.

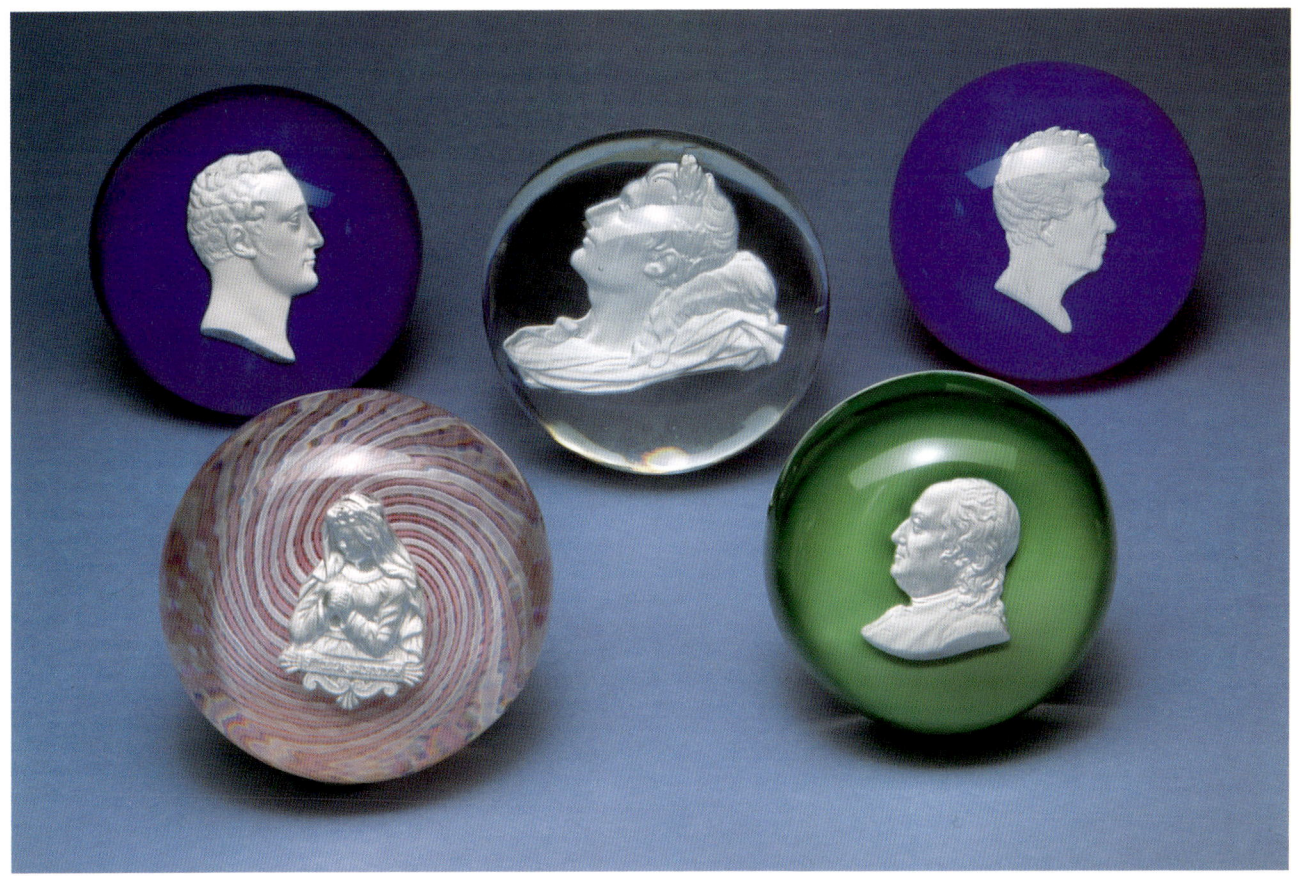

38. A paperweight with a profile portrait of Czar Nicholas I on an opaque blue ground. Clichy, circa 1840.

39. A paperweight, the clear ground with the death mask of Napoléon I resting in a cushion from a medal by Depaulis. Baccarat, circa 1821.
Literature: Jokelson, *Sulphides*, p. 94, fig. 96. Albert C. Revi, *Nineteenth Century Glass*, p. 280.

40. A paperweight with portrait profile of François René, vicomte de Chateaubriand (1768–1848) on an opaque blue ground. Clichy, circa 1840.

41. A paperweight with portrait of St. Elizabeth on a pink and white swirl ground. Clichy, circa 1840.

42. A paperweight with portrait profile of Benjamin Franklin (1706–1790) on an opaque apple-green ground. Clichy, circa 1840.

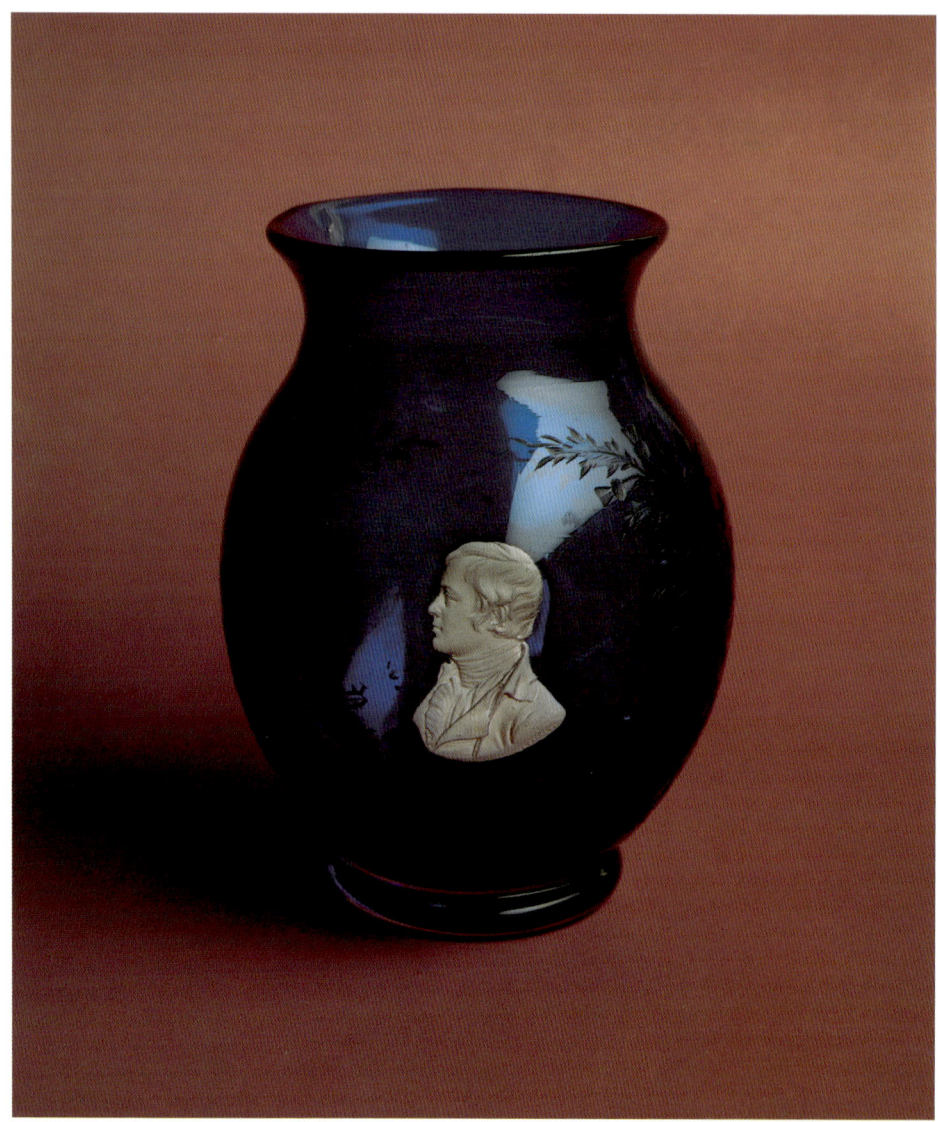

43. A translucent royal blue vase with portrait medallion of Robert Burns (1759–1796), engraved with foliate sprays. Inscription: *Robert Burns, Scotland's Bard, Born 25th January 1759*. The sulphide is signed *Moore* in the truncation. John Ford and Company, circa 1850.

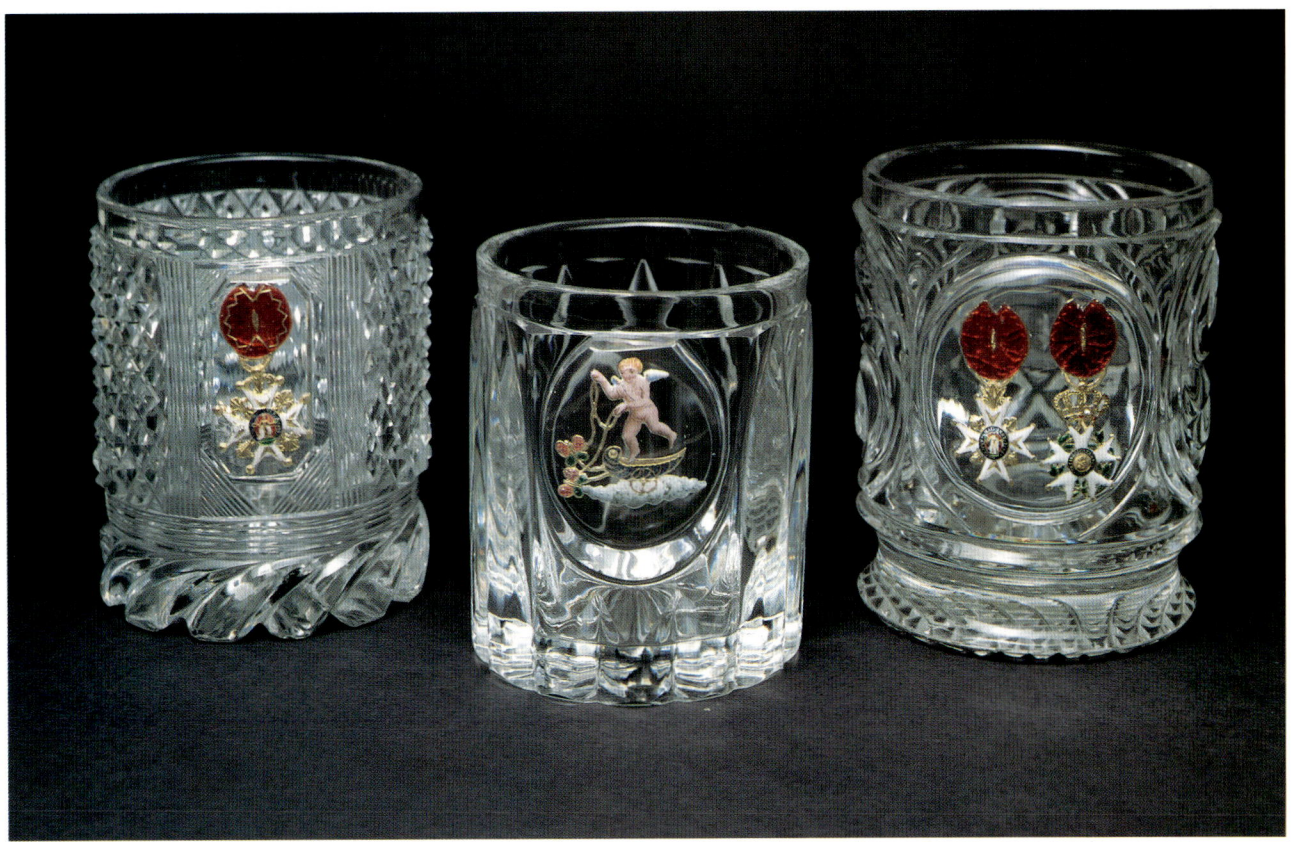

44. An enameled foil armorial tumbler decorated in colors with two coats of arms, depicting the Legion of Honor and Croix de Saint Louis within an oval cartouche. Baccarat, circa 1835.
Exhibited: Baccarat Antique Tumblers 1810–1860 (a traveling exhibit from Baccarat New York in 1986), no. 3.

45. A tumbler decorated in enameled foil colors depicting Cupid on a shell driven by butterflies, within an oval cartouche. Baccarat, circa 1820–1840.
Exhibited: Baccarat Antique Tumblers 1810–1860, no. 49.

46. An enameled foil armorial tumbler decorated in colors depicting the Croix de Saint Louis within an octagonal cartouche. Baccarat, circa 1835.
Exhibited: Baccarat Antique Tumblers 1810–1860, no. 8.

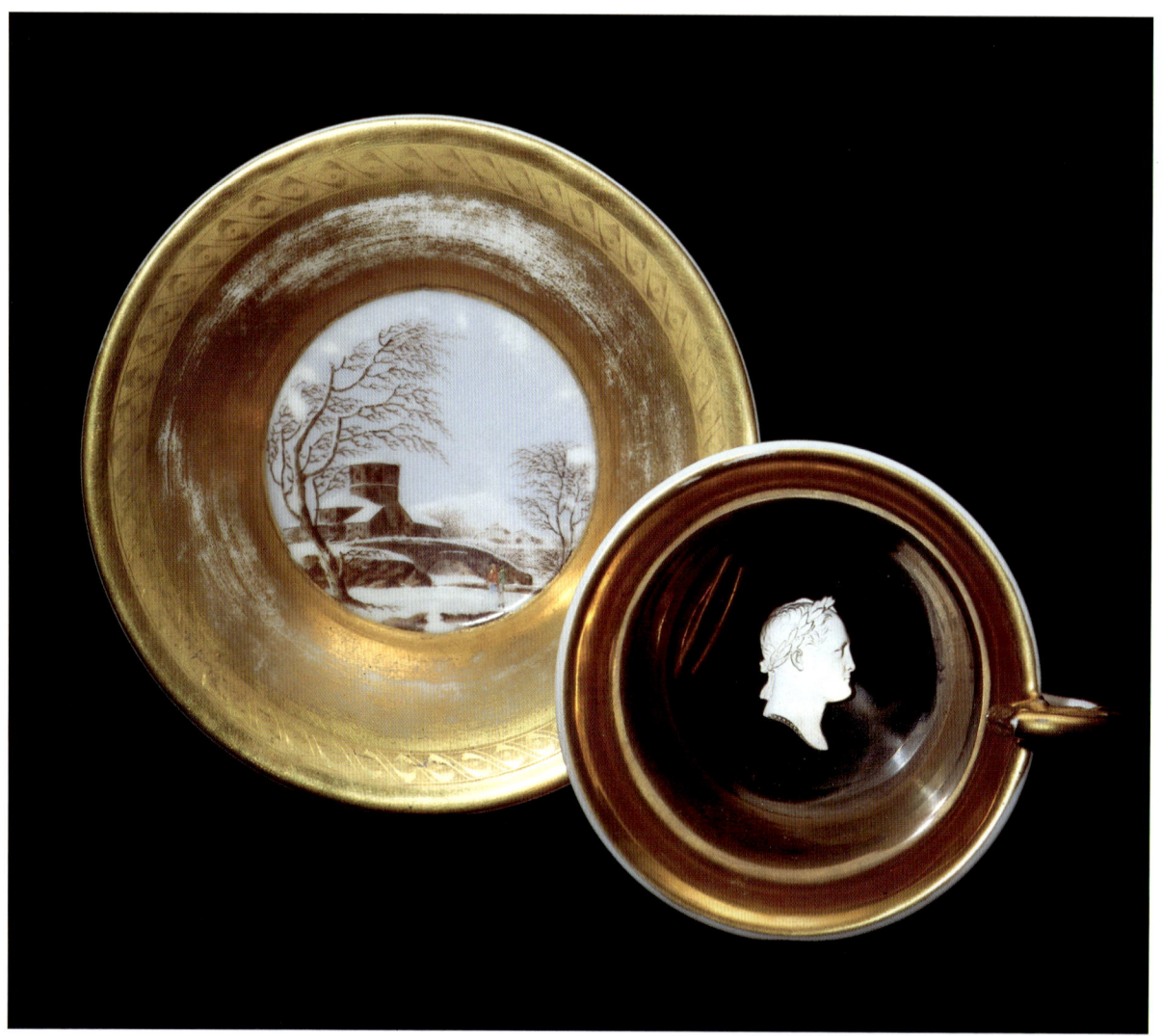

47. A cup with matching saucer, the profile portrait of Czar Nicholas I in the base of the cup signed *Andrieu* in the truncation, the reverse marked *Desprez, /Rue des Récolets/No. 2, à Paris*, enameled and gilded, with a transfer-printed Russian winter scene on saucer. Sèvres, France, circa 1820.

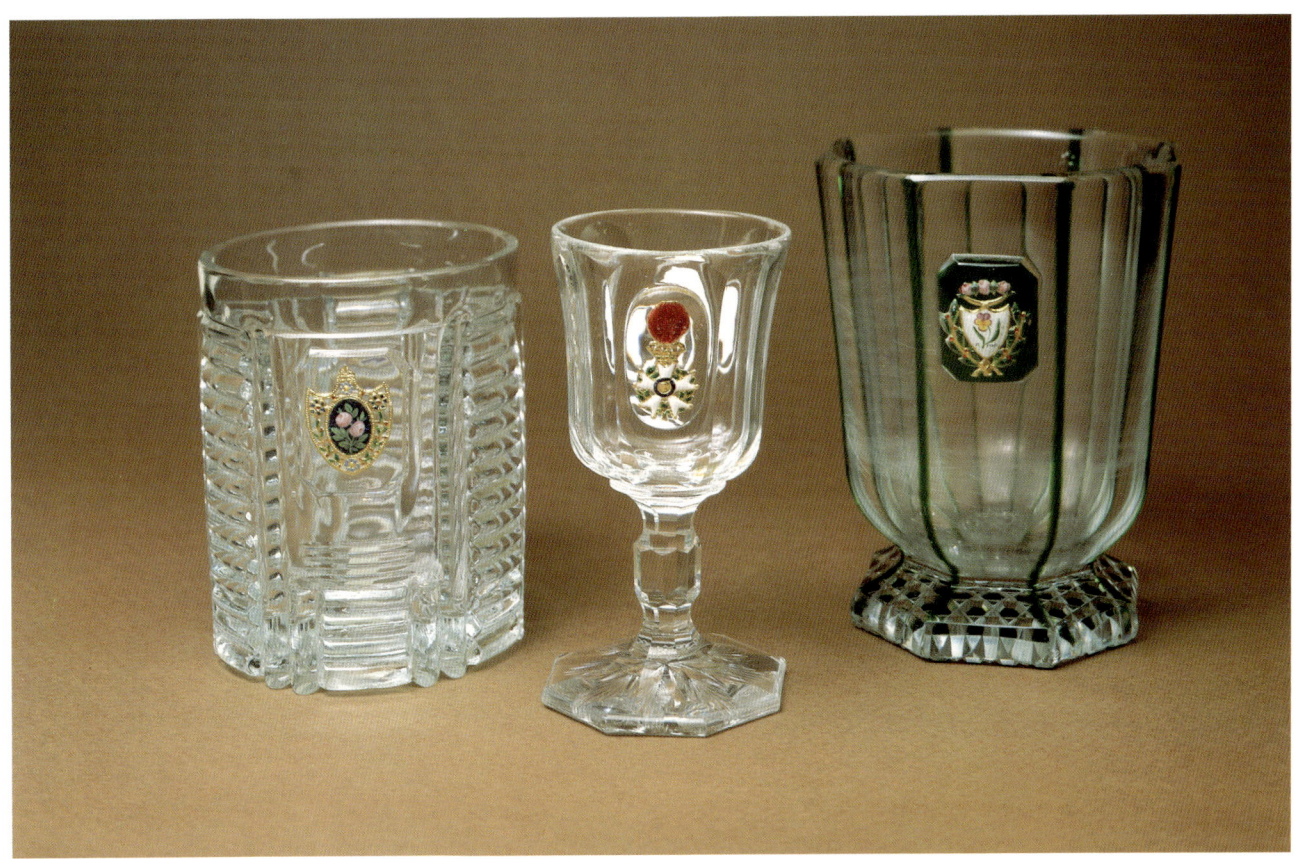

48. An enameled gold foil tumbler, the central medallion containing a gold crest with roses. Baccarat, circa 1820–1830.
Exhibited: Baccarat Antique Tumblers 1810–1860, no. 51.

49. An enameled foil goblet containing a profile portrait of Napoléon I by Andrieu, the reverse containing an inclusion of the Legion of Honor. Baccarat, circa 1825–1835.
Exhibited: Baccarat Antique Tumblers 1810–1860, no. 2.

50. An enameled gold foil tumbler with green flash overlay, the central medallion containing flowers with a pansy, inscribed *à moi*. The meaning is *pensez à moi* (think of me), since the word *pensée* (pansy) sounds like the word *pensez* (think). Saint Louis [?], circa 1820–1830.
Exhibited: Baccarat Antique Tumblers 1810–1860, no. 46.

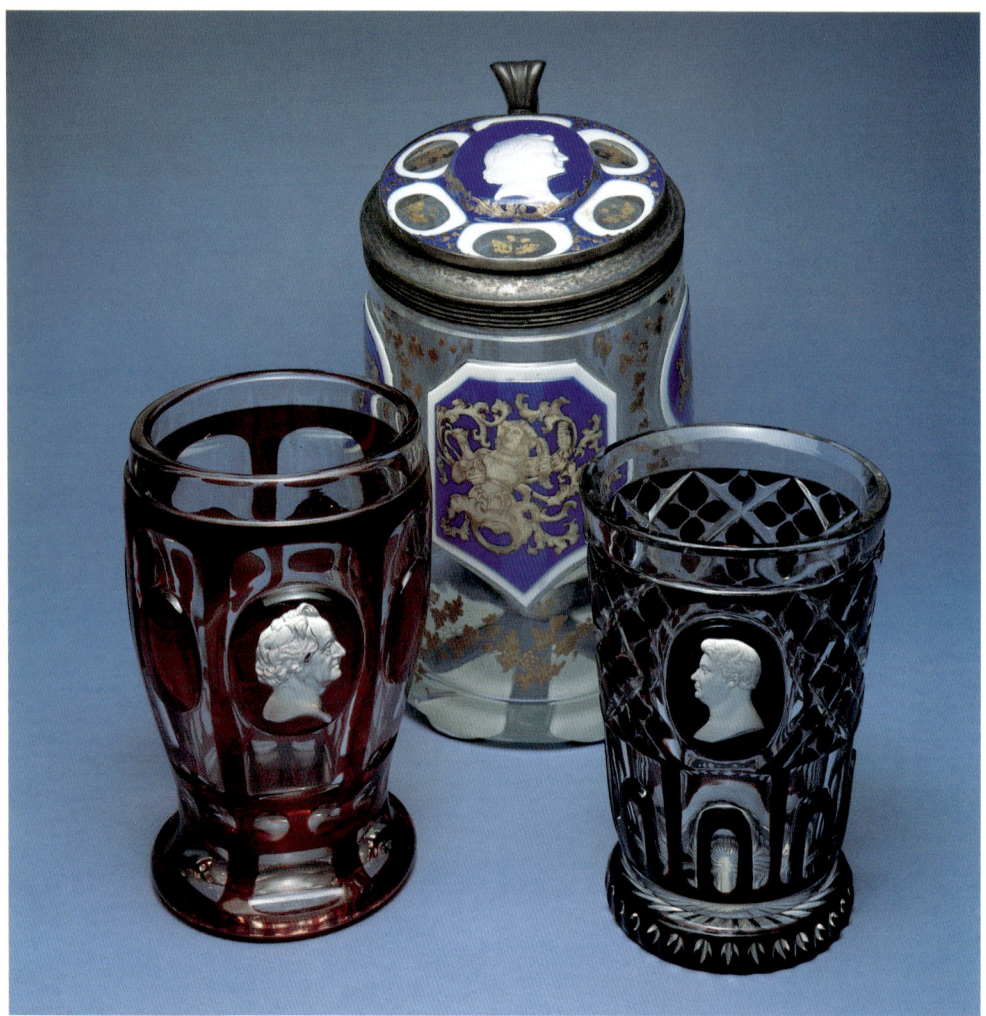

51. A tankard, the clear glass with opaque blue and white double overlay, enclosing a portrait profile of Friedrich von Schiller (1759–1805) on the lid, gilt scroll and vine decoration. Bohemian, circa 1840.

52. A North Bohemian beaker, the whole overlaid with translucent ruby, containing an oval medallion with ruby ground enclosing a profile portrait of Johann Wolfgang von Goethe (1749–1832). Bohemia, circa 1835.
Literature: Jokelson, *Sulphides,* plate IX.

53. A North Bohemian beaker, the flared sides overlaid in translucent ruby, cut through with deeper florets and ovals around an oval medallion with ruby ground, enclosing a portrait profile of Friedrich Wilhelm IV of Prussia (1795–1861). Inscribed *W. Kirchner F.* on truncation. Hurrach Glassworks, Neuwelt, circa 1830.
Provenance: Fritz Biemann Collection, Lucerne
Literature: Klesse, Saldren, *500 Jahre Glaskunst,* p. 267, plate 236.

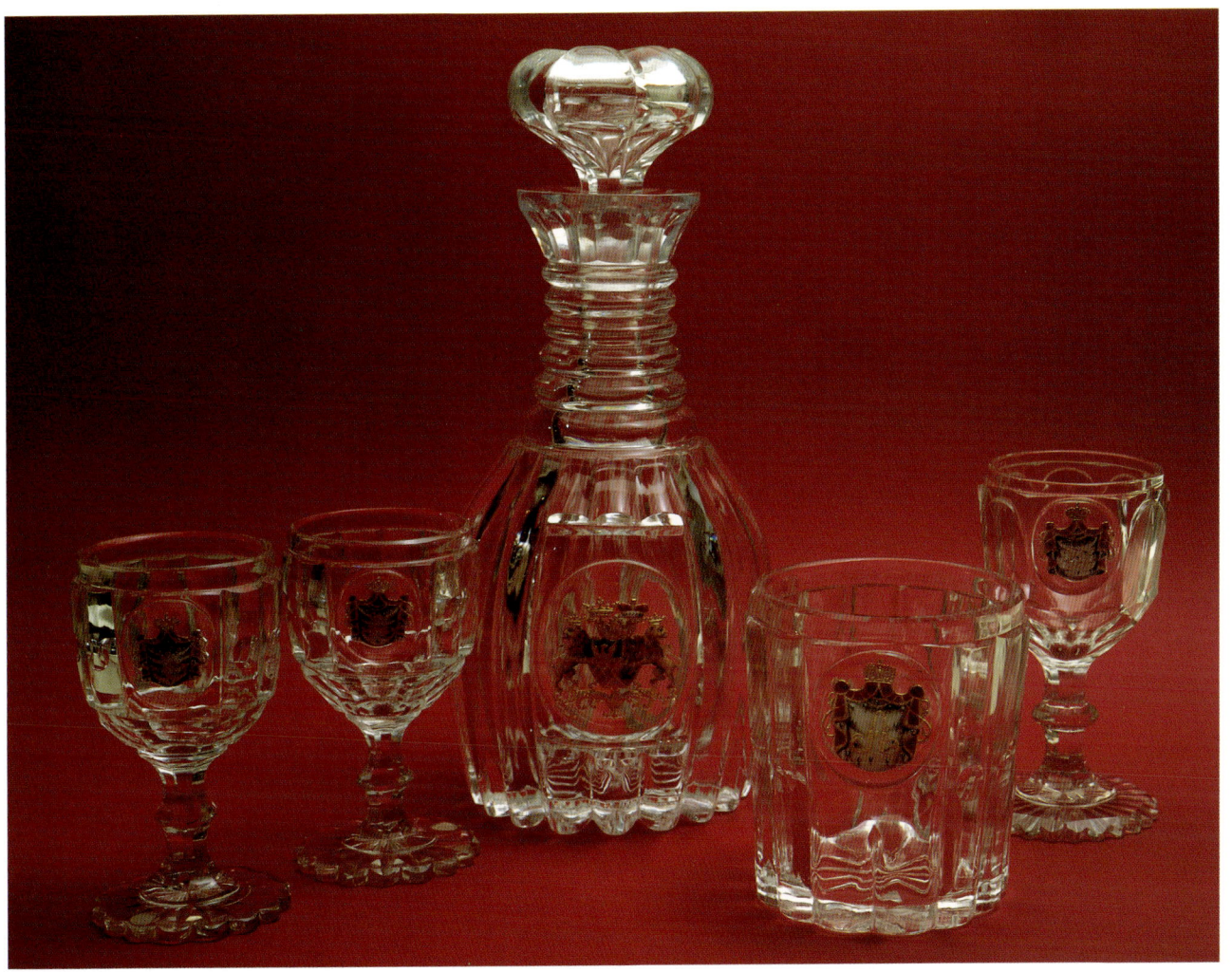

54. A pair of goblets with enameled foil inclusions bearing the initial "A" on a crowned ermine mantle, signifying Czar Alexander I (1777–1825). Imperial Glass Factory, Russia, circa 1825.

55. A decanter and stopper with an enameled foil inclusion from the Naryshkin service, the cut decanter containing an elaborate armorial with hollow stopper; presented by Czar Alexander I to Madame Naryshkin upon her marriage to Prince Svyatopolk. Imperial Glass Factory, Russia, circa 1823.

56. A tumbler with an enameled foil inclusion, cut and bearing the initial "A" on a crowned ermine mantle, signifying Czar Alexander I. Imperial Glass Factory, Russia, circa 1825.

57. A goblet with an enameled foil inclusion bearing the monogram "AN" for Alexander Nikolaievich, on a crowned ermine mantle. Cut and made for the Imperial Banqueting Service. Imperial Glass Factory, Russia, circa 1880.

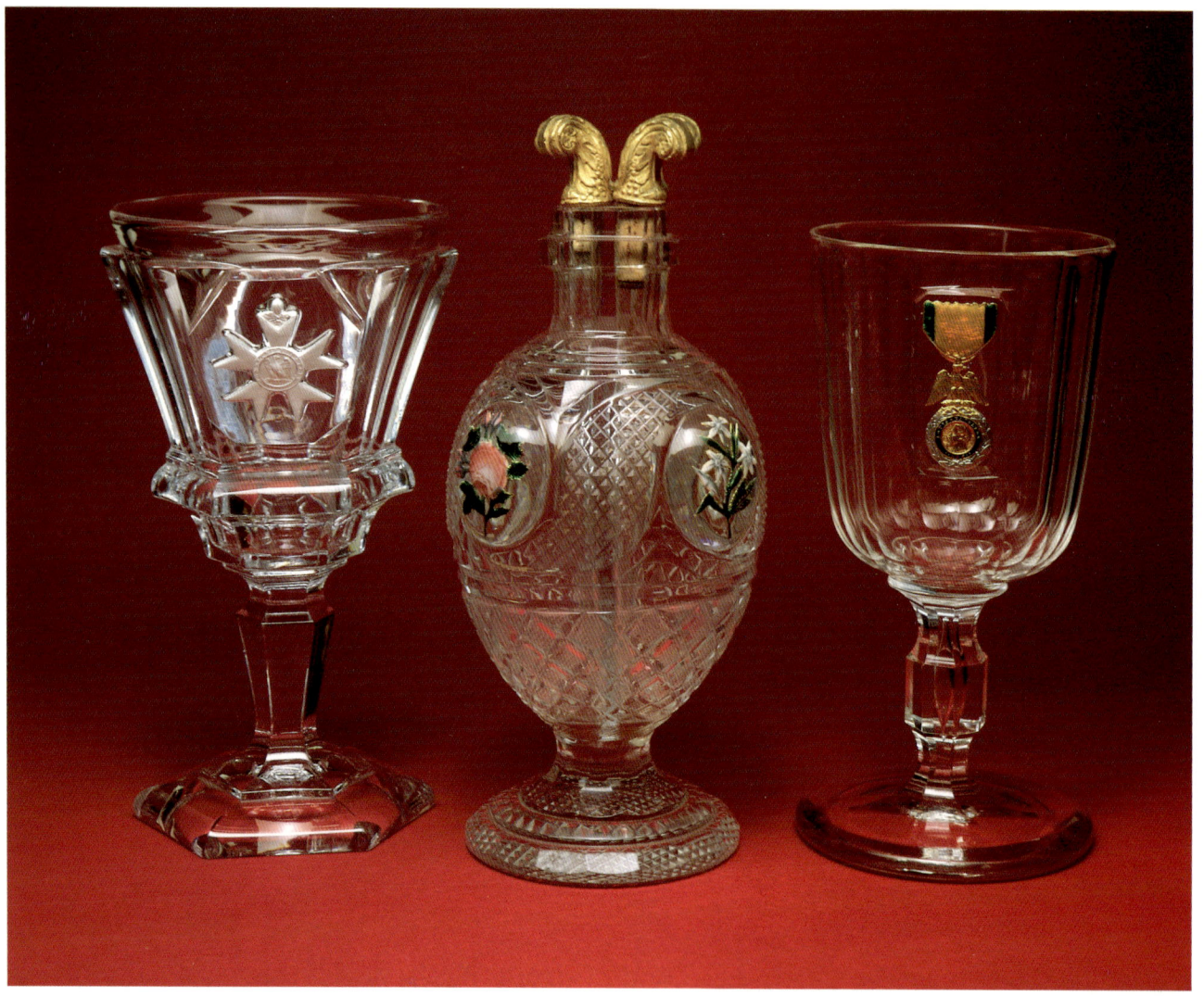

58. An enameled foil goblet, the central medallion containing the Médaille Militaire, created on January 22, 1852 by Napoléon III. It depicts the profile of Napoléon III crowned by a gold eagle with a yellow ribbon. Baccarat, circa 1852.

59. A sectional enameled foil scent bottle containing four partitions enclosing inclusions of a rose, orange, violet, and narcissus, each terminating with gilt stoppers; apparently constructed in this manner to contain the essence of each flower. Baccarat, circa 1820–1830.

60. A goblet, the central medallion containing a medal inscribed *Honneur et Patrie.* Baccarat, circa 1820–1830.

61. A decanter and stopper, the central medallion enclosing a profile portrait of Caroline Bonaparte (1782–1839), signed *Andrieu*. It is interesting to note the use of a French sulphide in the production of another country. This was a frequent practice among manufacturers. John Ford Company, Edinburgh, circa 1870.
Literature: Jokelson, *Sulphides*, p. 119, fig. 104.

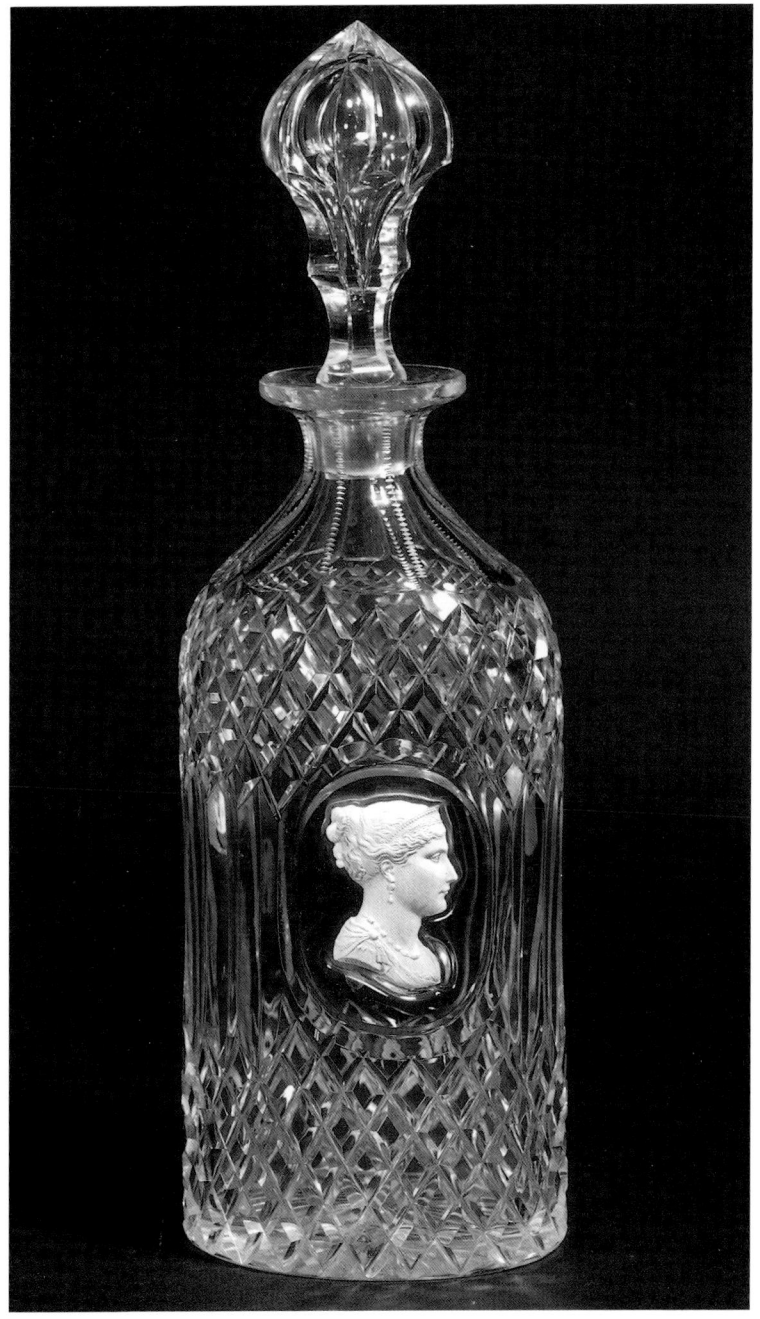

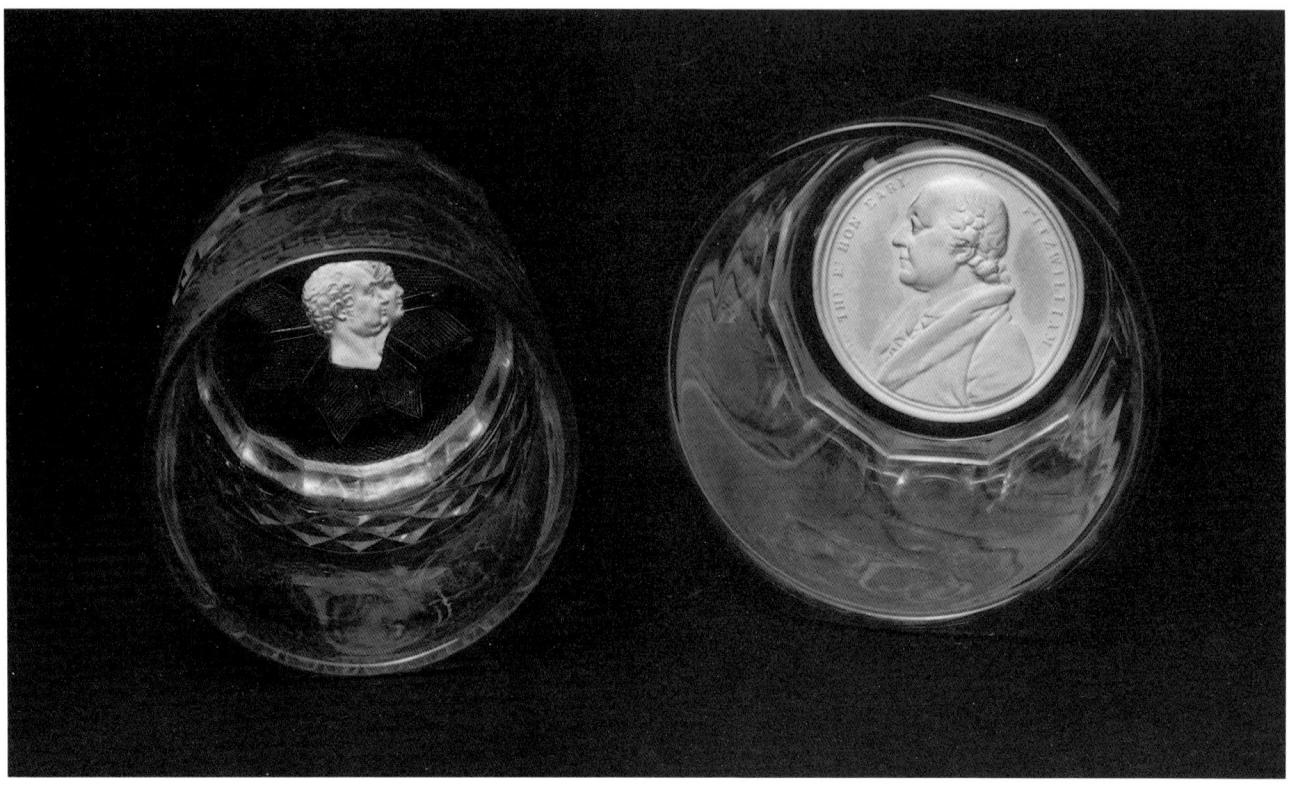

62. A tumbler, the base containing conjoined profile portraits, possibly Leopold II and Isabella of Parma, the straight-sided body decorated with delicate engraving. North Bohemian, possibly Franz Anton Riedel, circa 1825.

63. A tumbler, the base containing a portrait medallion of Charles William, 5th Earl Fitzwilliam (1786–1830), signed *Wilson*. The monogram on side is probably for the recipient. English, circa 1830.

Opposite page:

64. A cut ovoid bowl with central portrait medallion of Prince Albert (1819–1861), flanked by panels, diamonds and vertical blazes; sliced stem, foot with star-cut base. John Ford and Company, Edinburgh, circa 1850.

65. A ship's decanter and stopper, the spreading body with a named profile portrait of Robert Burns, impressed on shoulder *J. Moore*, the reverse with a profile head of Shakespeare, both engraved with foliate sprays. The body is cut with vertical panels of diamonds. The base is star-cut; the neck is cut with facets, and the globular stopper is also faceted. John Ford and Company, Edinburgh, circa 1870.

66. A vase with two central portrait medallions of Queen Victoria, engraved with foliate sprays, sun-ray base. This is apparently an unfinished product, due to the imperfection in one of the sulphides. Ford and Company, Edinburgh, circa 1850.
For a finished version, see Selman, *Paperweights for Collectors*, p. 95, fig. 201, no. 4.

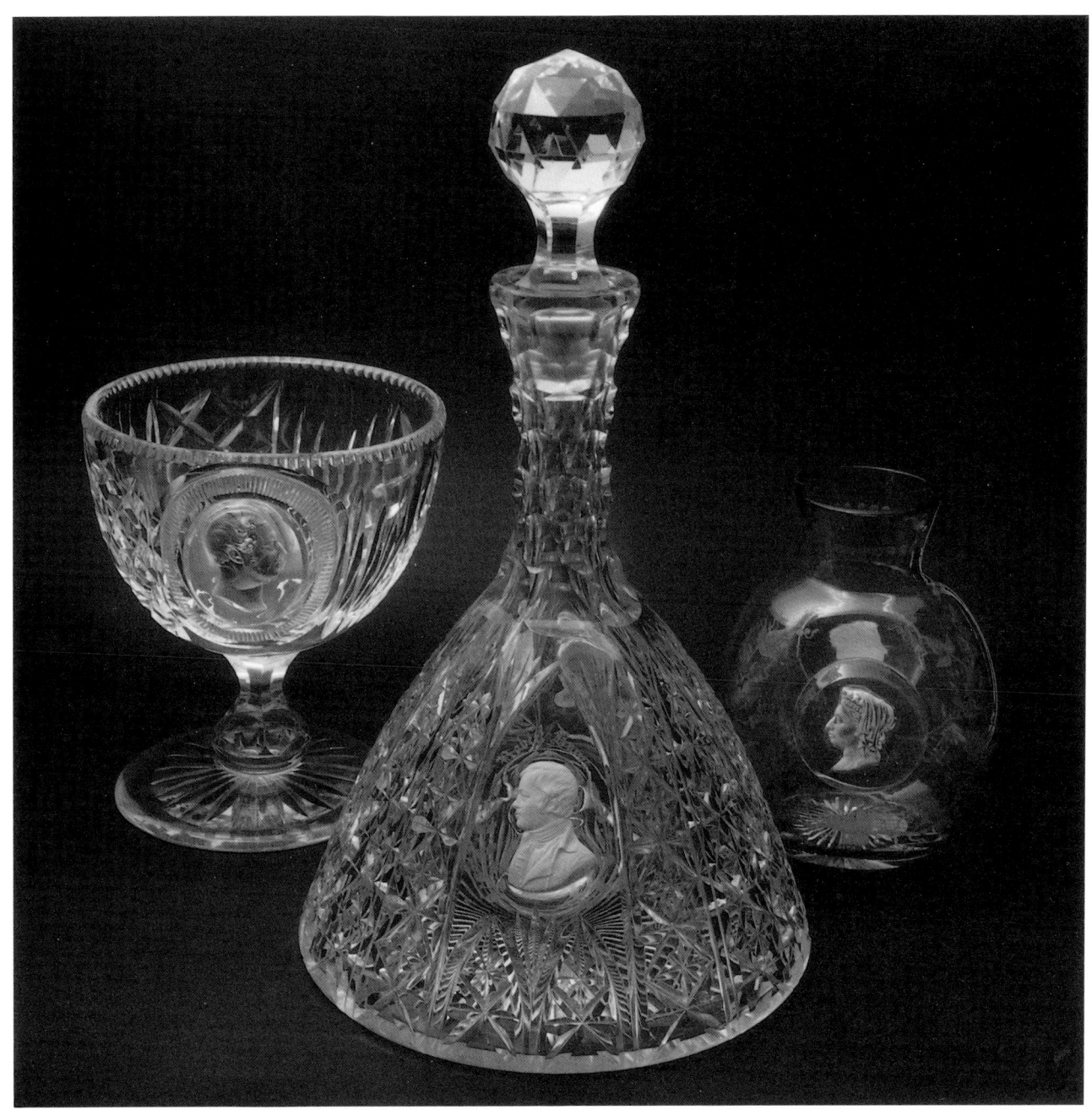

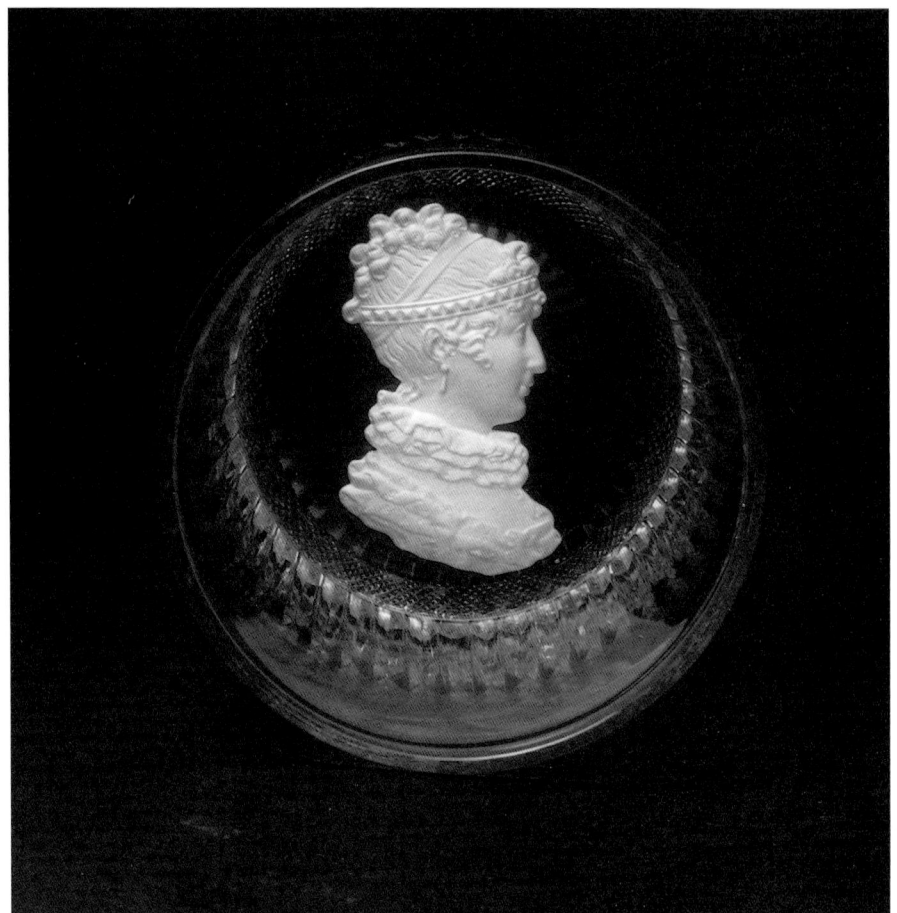

67. A tumbler, the base containing a profile portrait of the Duchesse d'Angoulême. Baccarat, circa 1820. Exhibited: Baccarat Antique Tumblers 1810–1860, no. 14.

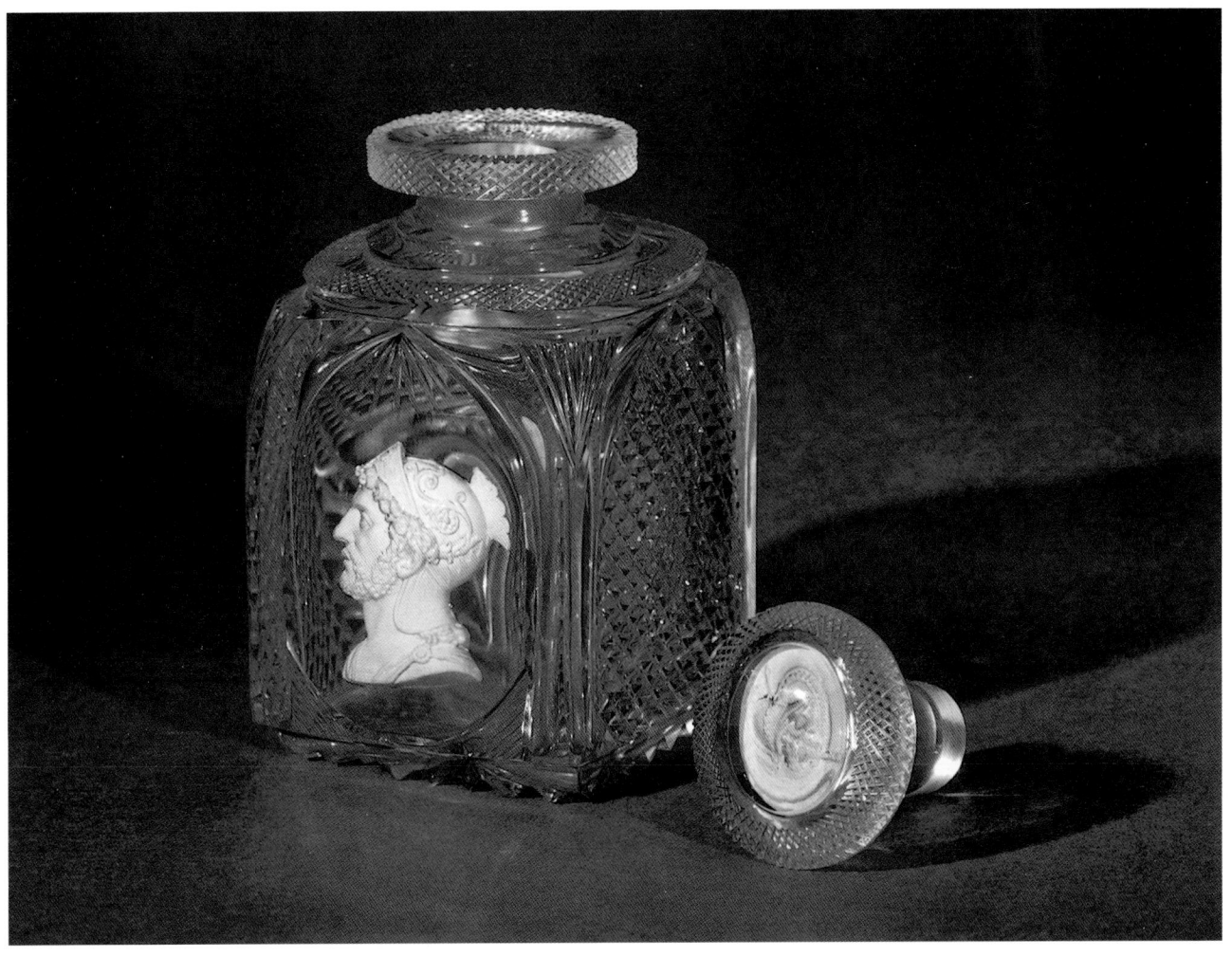

68. A toilet bottle, the central medallion enclosing a profile portrait of Pompey, the reverse enclosing a colored landscape, the stopper with allegorical figure. Apsley Pellatt, circa 1820.

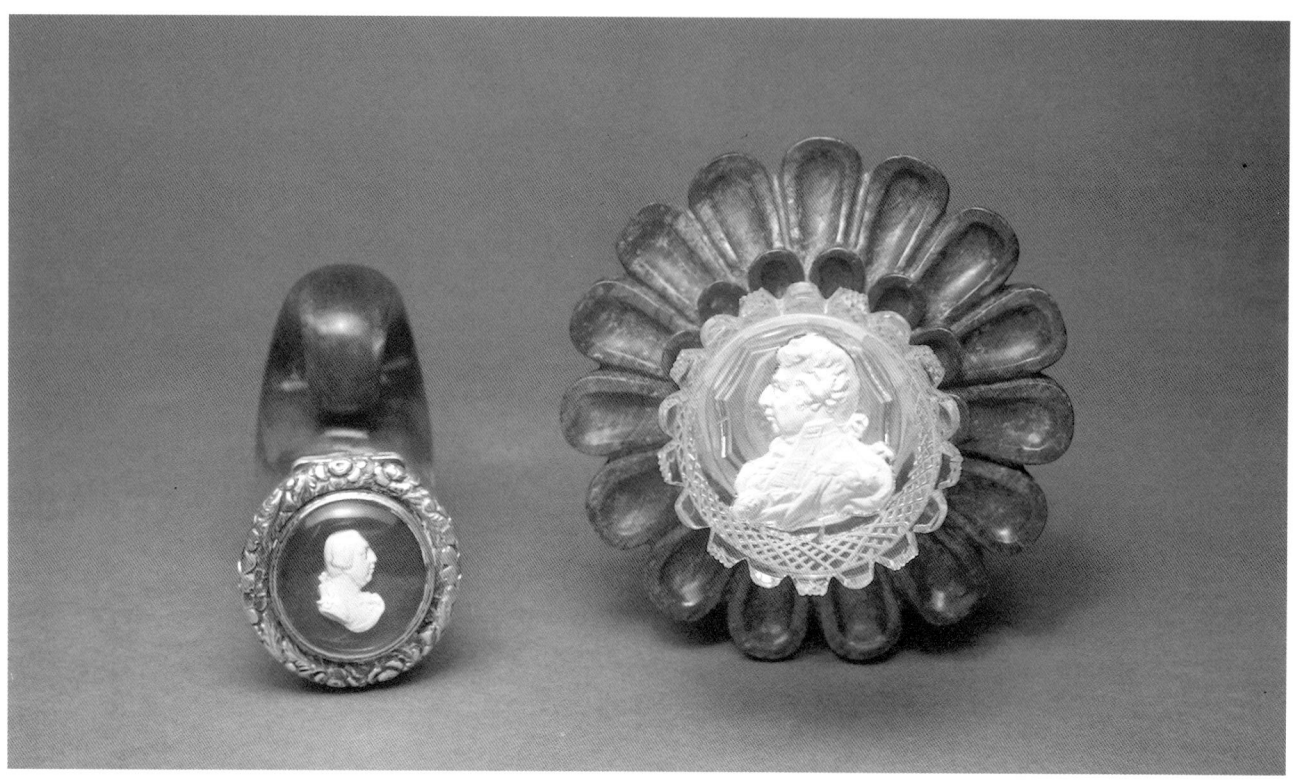

69. A snuff mull, the water buffalo horn capped by a profile portrait of George IV encased in a silver mounting. Apsley Pellatt, circa 1815.

70. A doorknob, enclosing a profile portrait of George III, with hobnail and diamond-cutting, together with its original wooden mounting. Apsley Pellatt, circa 1820.

Opposite page:

71. A mantel ornament, the medallion set with a profile portrait of Queen Victoria, entirely cut in typical Anglo-Irish style. Apsley Pellatt, circa 1840–1860.

72. A mantel ornament, the medallion set with a profile portrait of the Duke of Wellington, entirely cut in typical Anglo-Irish style, similar to the preceding ornament. Apsley Pellatt, circa 1840–1860.

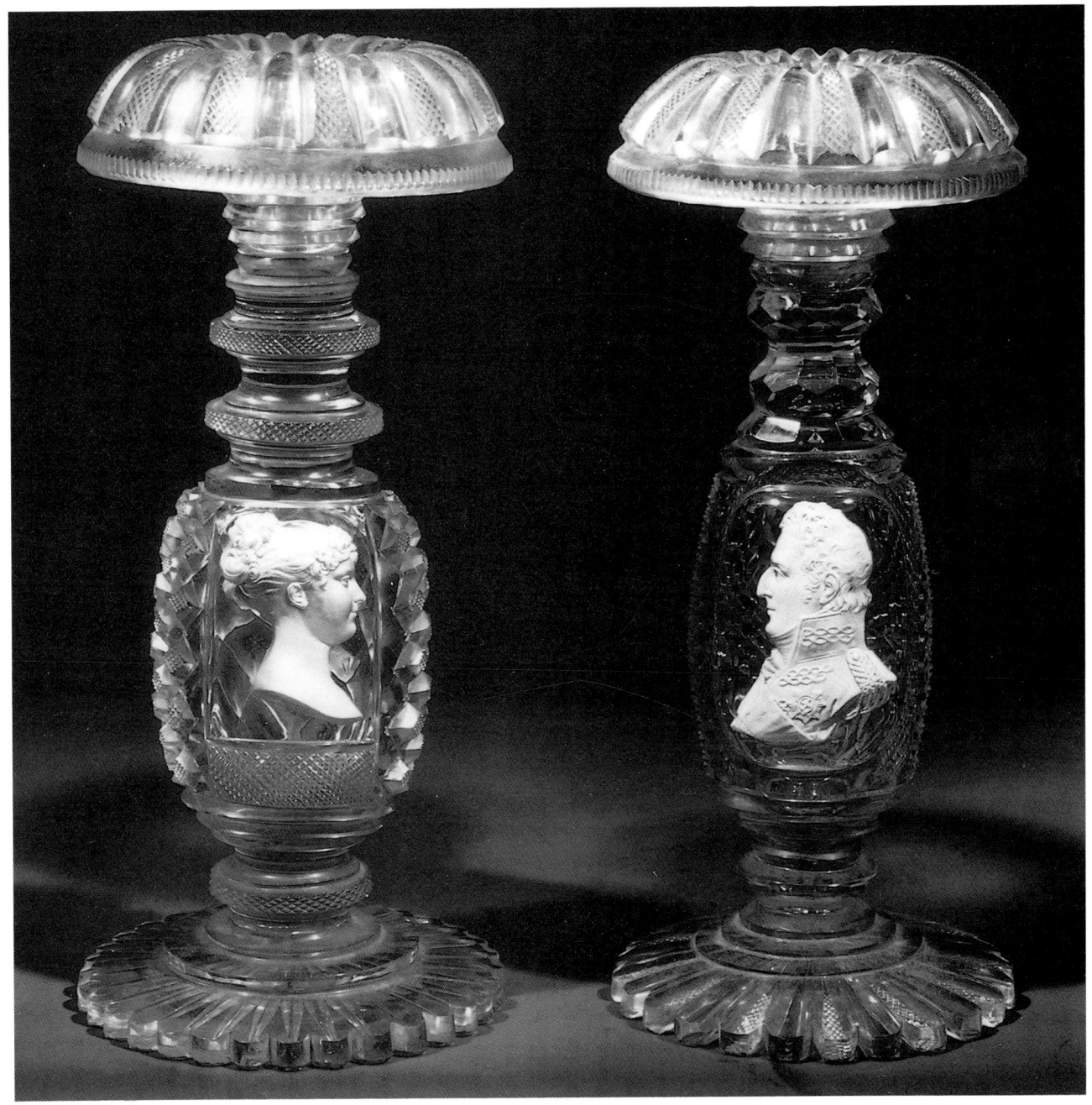

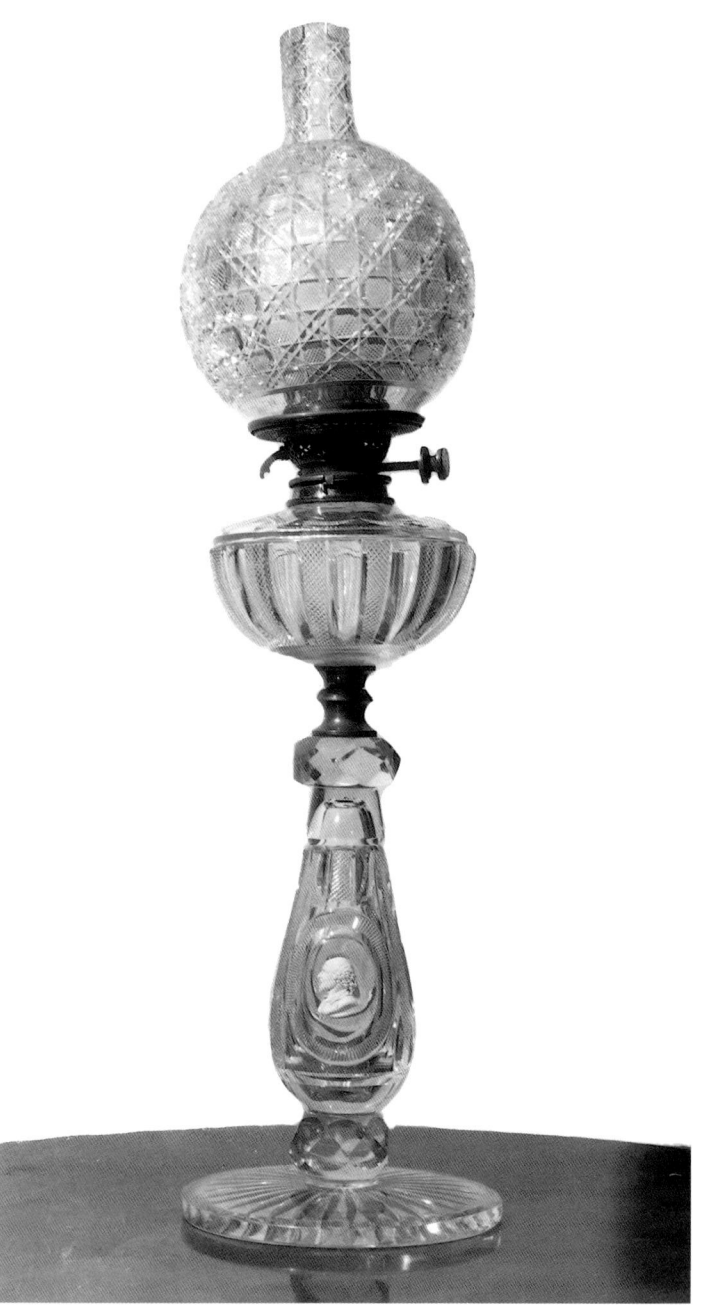

73. An extremely rare kerosene lamp, with profile portraits of William Shakespeare and Robert Burns. The portrait of Shakespeare was modeled by William Hackwood, one of the chief modelers for Wedgwood. The lamp is complete with elaborately cut chimney and shade. John Ford and Company, Edinburgh, circa 1870. The Sinumbra lamp illustrated in Pellatt, *Memoir . . . of Glass Manufactures*, plate E, fig. 11, may have served as an inspiration for this form.

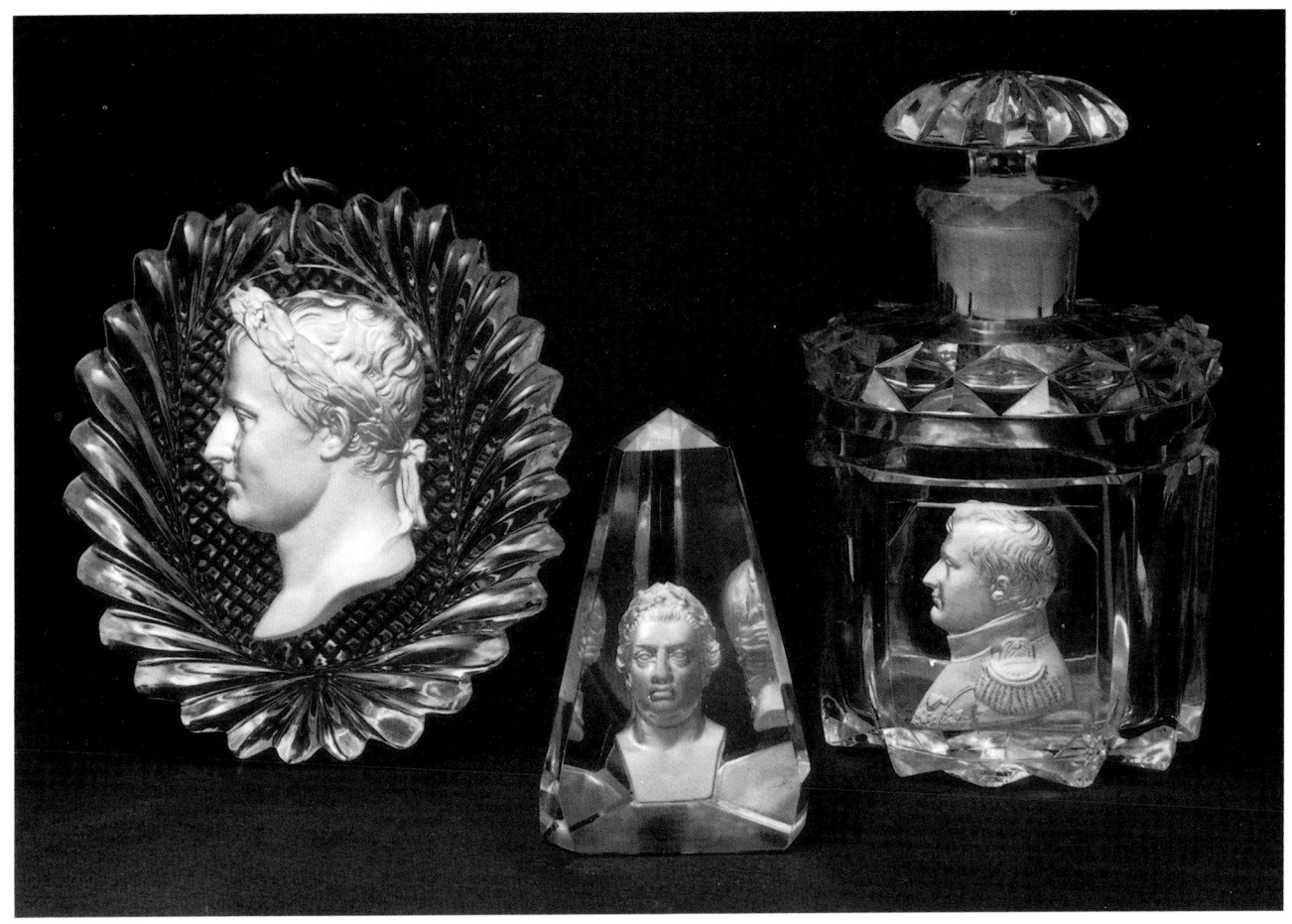

74. A plaque, the portrait profile of Napoléon I by Andrieu. Baccarat, circa 1820.

75. An obelisk enclosing the dimensional portrait of a man, probably George IV. The cameo is possibly of steatite composition. Baccarat, circa 1830.

76. A flacon, the clear glass enclosing a portrait profile of Napoléon I in the uniform of the Colonel de la Garde, by Andrieu. Baccarat, circa 1824.

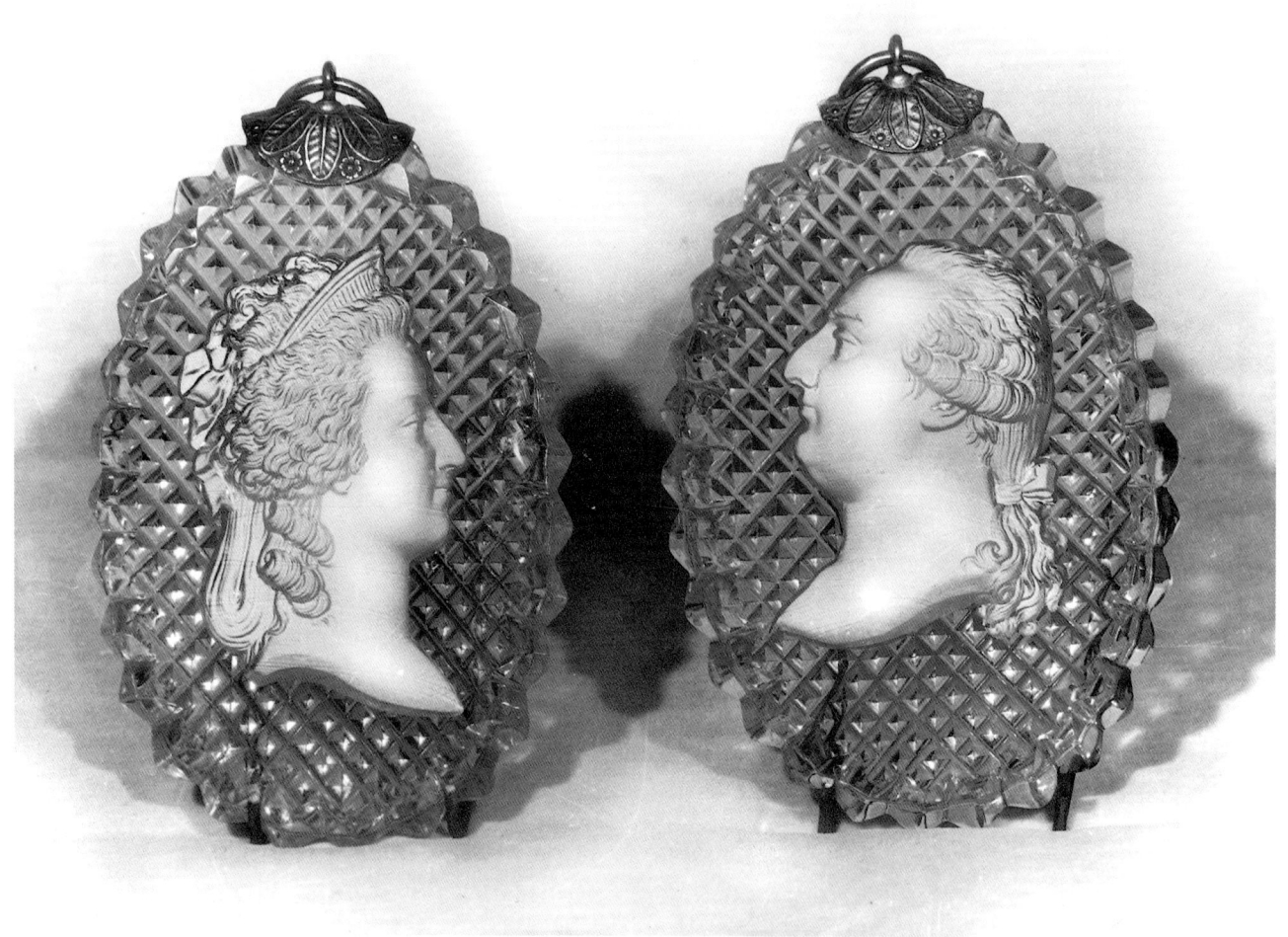

77. A plaque enclosing a portrait profile of Queen Marie-Antoinette (1755–1793), after a medal by Pierre Duvivier, diamond cutting on reverse. Baccarat, circa 1820–1840.
Literature: Jokelson, *Sulphides*, p. 88, fig. 88.

78. A plaque enclosing a portrait profile of King Louis XVI of France (1754–1793), after a medal by J. P. Droz, diamond cutting on reverse. Baccarat, circa 1820–1840.
Literature: Jokelson, *Sulphides*, p. 88, fig. 88.

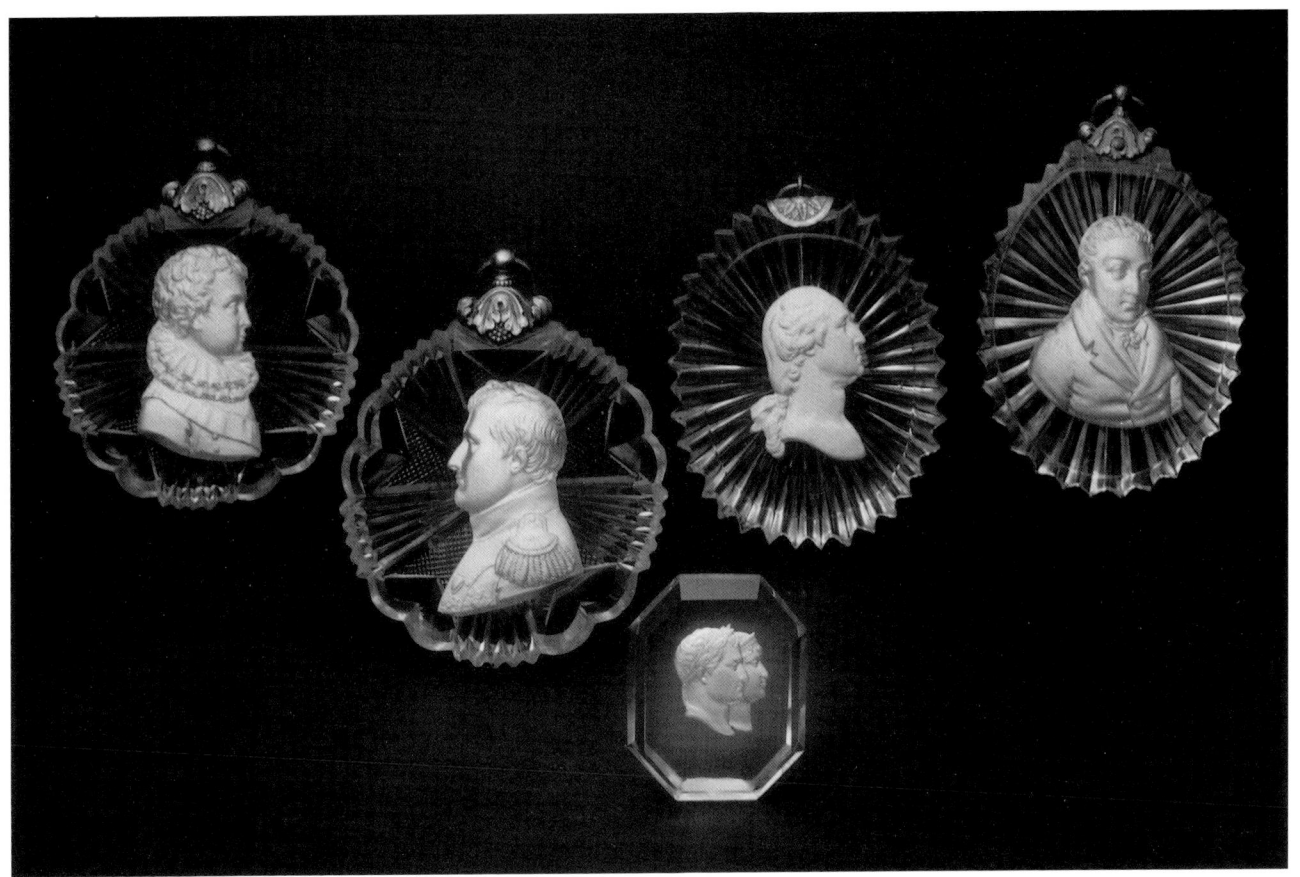

79. A portrait plaque enclosing a portrait profile of Napoléon II; the reverse is cut in the motif of the Legion of Honor. Baccarat, circa 1825.

80. A portrait plaque enclosing a portrait profile of Napoléon I in the uniform of the Colonel de la Garde. The reverse is cut in the motif of the Legion of Honor. Baccarat, circa 1820.

81. A plaque enclosing a profile portrait of George Washington by Martoret, from a medal by Duvivier, radial cutting on reverse. Baccarat, circa 1820.

82. A plaque enclosing a portrait of General Lafayette, after the bronze bust presented to President Monroe. Lafayette was a guest of the United States in 1824 and 1825. The bust is now in the library of the James Monroe Memorial Foundation. Baccarat, circa 1825.

83. A portrait plaque enclosing a conjoined profile portrait of Napoléon and Josephine by Andrieu, dated *1810* on reverse. Baccarat, circa 1810.

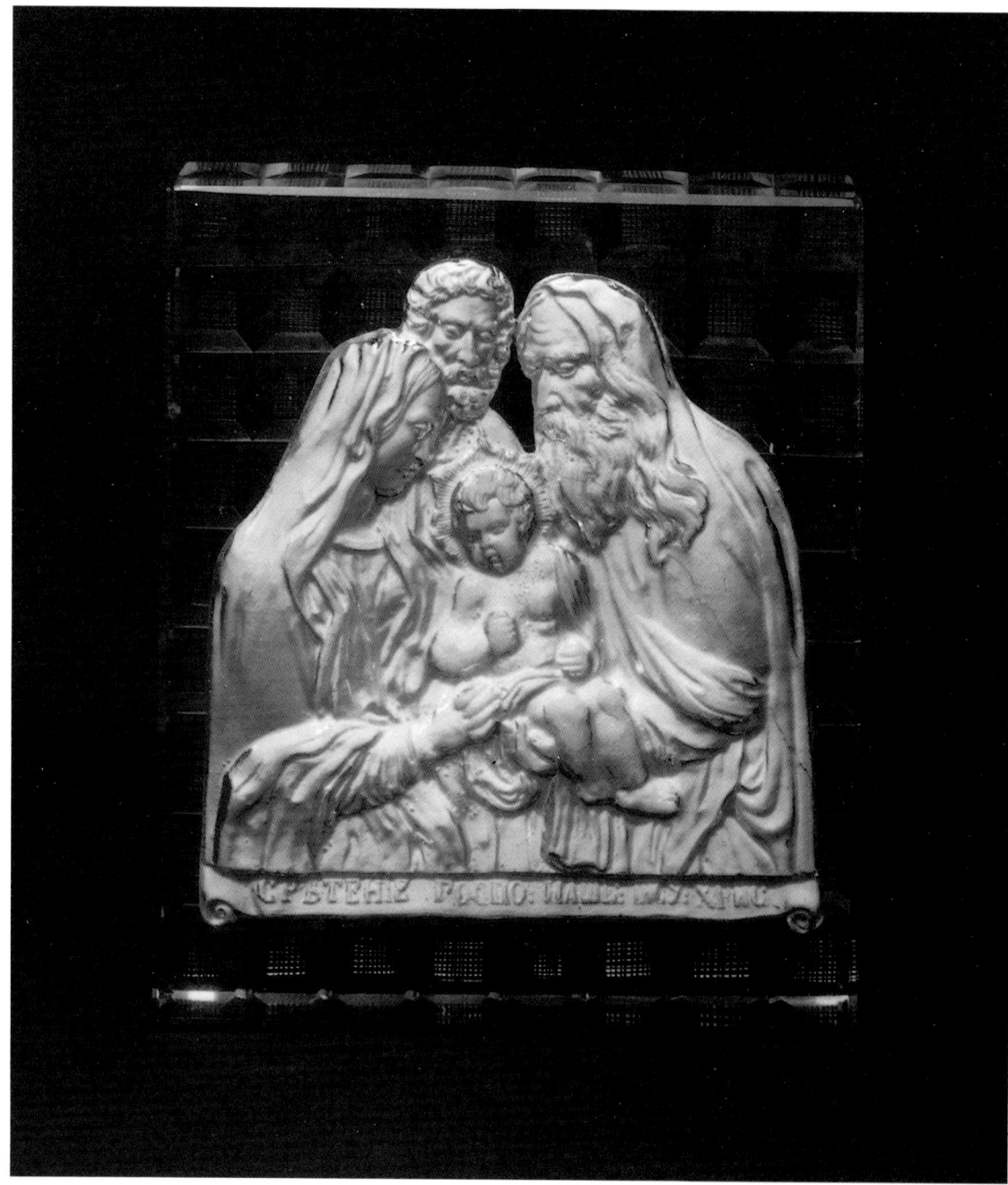

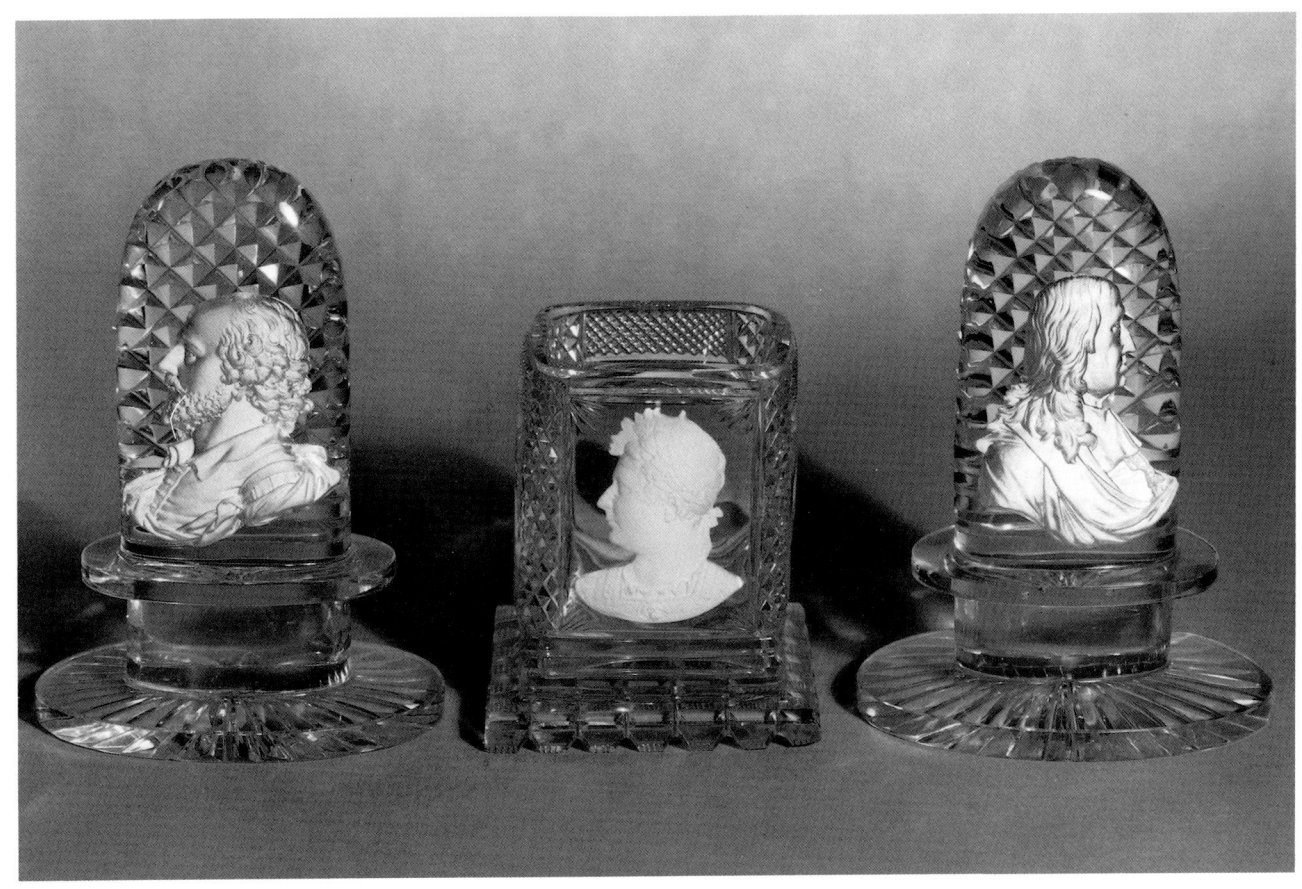

85. An ornament enclosing a medallion of William Shakespeare, the stepped top with diamond cutting on reverse. Apsley Pellatt, circa 1820.

86. A four-sided receptacle enclosing profile portraits of George IV, Queen Victoria, a basket of flowers and a putto figure. One sulphide is signed *Pellatt and Green*, the other *Patent, London.* Apsley Pellatt, circa 1840–1860.

87. An ornament enclosing a medallion of John Milton, the stepped top with diamond cutting on reverse, from a medal by John Sigismund Tanner. Apsley Pellatt, circa 1820.

Opposite page:

84. A portrait plaque depicting the Holy Family. The reverse contains a deep diamond cutting, bearing the inscription *God, Our Child Jesus* in Cyrillic. Stylistically, this plaque bears great similarity to the pair of portrait plaques in the collection of the Corning Museum, signed *Bakhmetief, Nikolskoie,* enclosing the portraits of Czar Nicholas I and Alexander II. Bakhmetief, Russia, circa 1855.

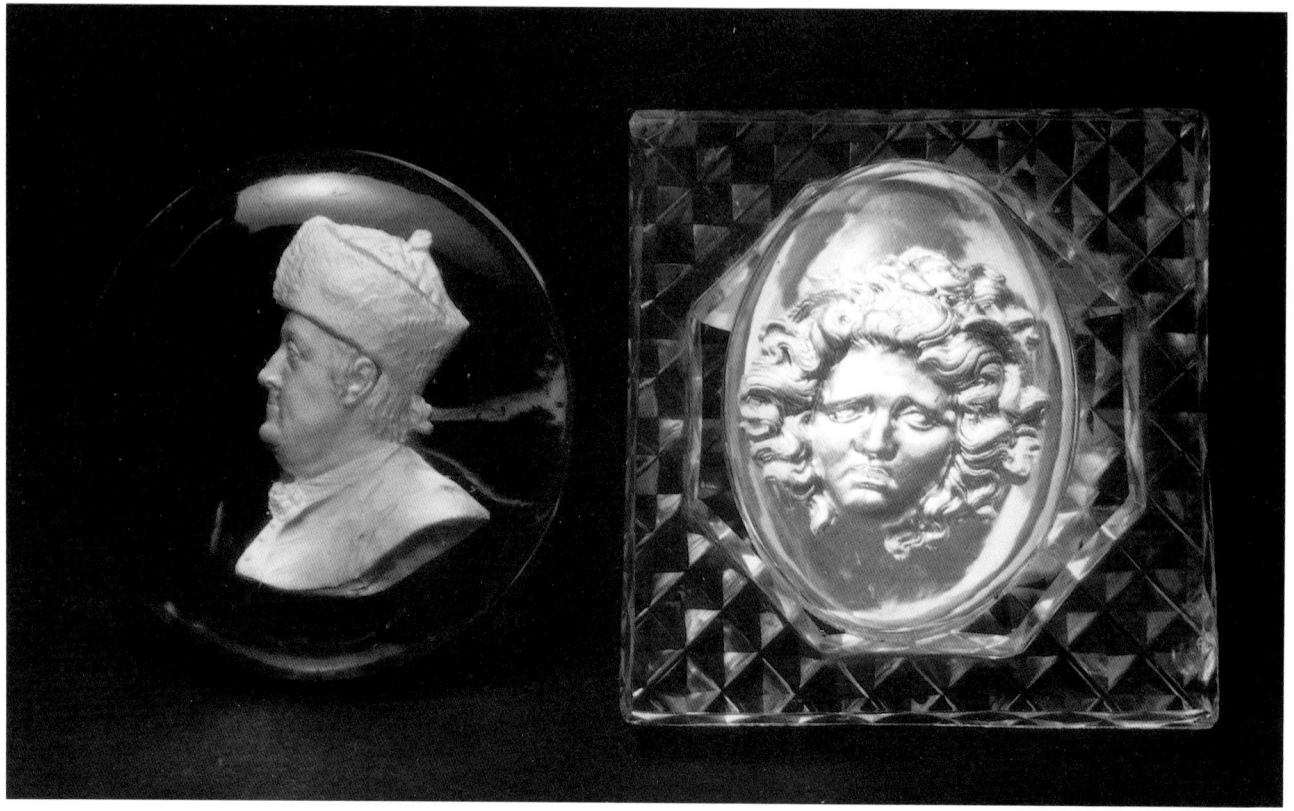

88. A circular plaque, the profile portrait of Benjamin Franklin from a terra-cotta by Jean-Baptiste Nini. French, Boudon de Saint-Amans, circa 1820.
Pierre Honoré Boudon de Saint-Amans secured a patent in 1818 for perfecting the process of encrusting cameos in glass.

89. A letter press, the stepped form enclosing the mask of Medusa, base diamond-cut. French, Boudon de Saint-Amans, circa 1820.

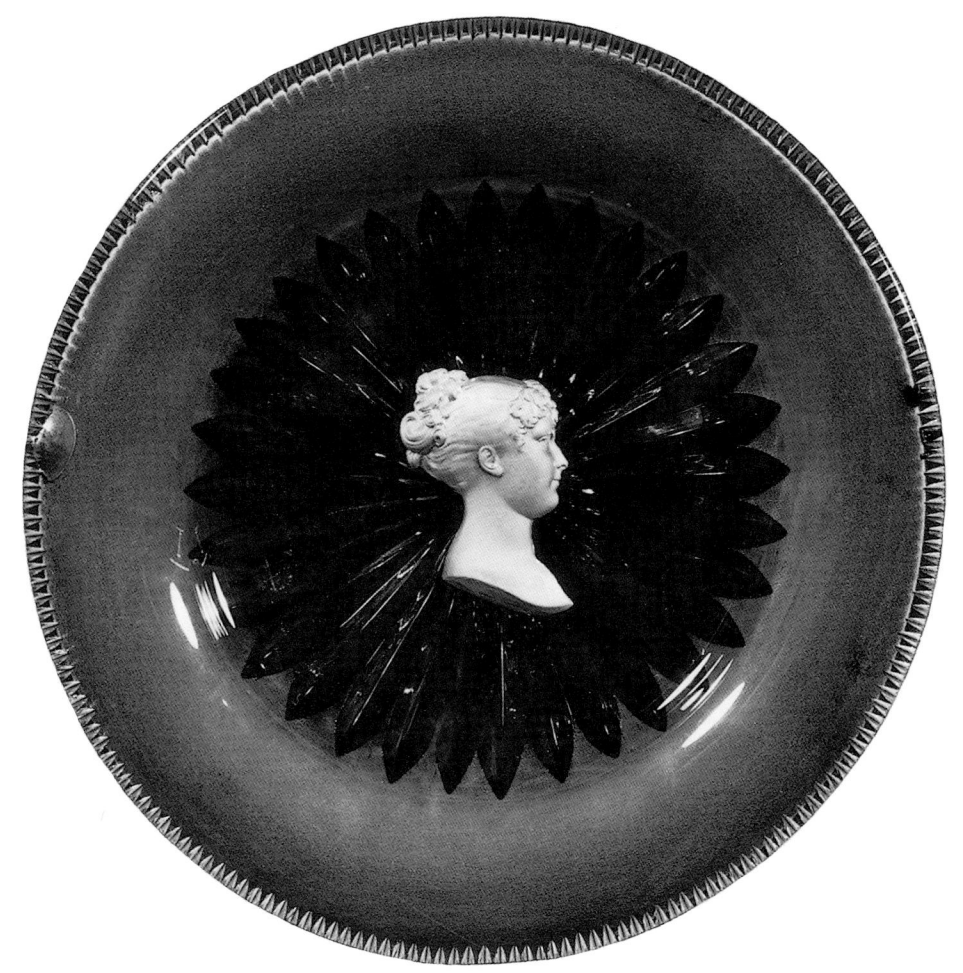

90. An ice plate, the central medallion enclosing a profile portrait of Queen Victoria. Apsley Pellatt, circa 1840–1860.
A similar plate illustrated in Pellatt, *Memoir . . . of Glass Manufactures,* fig. 20, plate G.

BIBLIOGRAPHY

Bohemian Glass, Victoria and Albert Museum. London, 1965.

Jokelson, Paul, *Antique French Paperweights.* [New York], 1955.

———, *Sulphides—The Art of Cameo Incrustation.* New York, 1968.

Kaminsky, Dena, "Sulphides: 'The Noble Simplicity and Quiet Grandeur'," *Annual Bulletin of the Paperweight Collectors' Association,* 1984, p. 30.

Klesse, Brigitte and Axel von Saldren, *500 Jahre Glaskunst.* Zurich, 1978.

Meteyard, Eliza, *Wedgwood and His Works.* London, 1873.

Pazaurek, Gustav E., *Gläser der Empire- und Biedermeierzeit.* Leipzig, 1923.

Pellatt, Apsley, *Memoir on the Origin, Progress, and Improvement of Glass Manufactures.* London, 1821.

———, *Curiosities of Glass Making,* London, 1849.

Reilly, Robin and George Savage, *Wedgwood—The Portrait Medallions.* London, 1973.

Revi, Albert Christian, *Nineteenth Century Glass.* New York, 1959; revised edition, 1967.

Selman, Lawrence H. and Linda Pope-Selman, *Paperweights for Collectors.* Santa Cruz, California, 1975.